SEMEIA 57

Discursive Formations, Ascetic Piety and the Interpretation of Early Christian Literature, Part 1

Editor:
Vincent L. Wimbush

©1992
by the Society of Biblical Literature

Published by
SCHOLARS PRESS
P.O. BOX 15399
Atlanta, GA 30333-0399

Printed in the United States of America
on acid free paper

CONTENTS

PART 1

Preface v

Contributors to This Issue vii

Introduction: *Vincent L. Wimbush* 1

I

1. The Case of the Blinking I: Discourse of the Self at Qumran
   Carol A. Newsom 13

2. Like Dogs Barking: Cynic *parrēsia* and Shameless Asceticism
   Leif E. Vaage 25

3. In Praise of Noble Women: Asceticism, Patronage and Honor
   Karen Jo Torjesen 41

4. The Defense of the Body and the Discourse of Appetite:
   Continence and Control in the Greco-Roman World
   Gail Paterson Corrington 65

II

5. Asceticism and Ideology: The Language of Power
   in the Pastoral Epistles
   Lucinda A. Brown 77

6. The Language of Desire: Clement of Alexandria's
   Transformation of Ascetic Discourse
   David G. Hunter 95

7. Allegory and Asceticism in Gregory of Nyssa
   Verna E. F. Harrison 113

8. The Body as Desert in *The Life of St. Anthony*
   Neal Kelsey 131

Glossary 153

Selected Bibliography: Asceticism and Discursive Strategies 157

Essays by the following will appear in Part 2, *Semeia* 58: Marilyn Nagy, James E. Goehring, Richard Valantasis, Vincent L. Wimbush, Virginia Burrus, and Jason David BeDuhn. There will also be a response to the collection, parts one and two, by Geoffrey Galt Harpham.

Preface

With this issue of *Semeia* a change in the cover will begin. It will take place gradually over the next several issues. We are grateful to Carole R. Fontaine, a member of the *Semeia* editorial board, for planning the art work for the change in the cover and also for the work on the individual covers on this and future issues.

Robert C. Culley
General Editor, *Semeia*

CONTRIBUTORS TO THIS ISSUE

Lucinda Brown
    Claremont Graduate School
    Claremont CA

Gail Paterson Corrington
    Rhodes College
    Memphis TN

Verna E. F. Harrison
    Berkeley CA

David G. Hunter
    University of St. Thomas
    St. Paul MN

Neal Kelsey
    Claremont Graduate School
    Claremont CA

Carol A. Newsom
    Candler School of Theology
    Emory University

Karen J. Torjeson
    Claremont Graduate School
    Claremont CA

Leif E. Vaage
    Emmanuel College
    University of Toronto
    Canada

RHETORICS OF RESTRAINT:
DISCURSIVE STRATEGIES, ASCETIC PIETY AND THE INTERPRETATION OF RELIGIOUS LITERATURE

INTRODUCTION

Vincent L. Wimbush
Union Theological Seminary
New York City

This collection of essays, spread over two consecutive volumes of *Semeia*, is the second major project of the Asceticism Group, a collaborative research project originally begun under auspices of the Institute for Antiquity and Christianity of Claremont, California. It is now known primarily as a program unit of the National Meetings of the American Academy of Religion/ Society of Biblical Literature, and in connection with the gratifying annual conversations and experiences of pre-national meetings' mini-conferences. (Most of the essays included in these two volumes were originally papers read as part of the November 1990 Asceticism Group Mini-Conference and AAR/SBL Program Unit Meeting in New Orleans.) Although there are important recent works of individual scholars that can be pointed to as indices of resurgent interest in asceticism in Greco-Roman antiquity and Jewish and Christian antiquity, the continuing conversation among the members of the Asceticism Group represents enormous potential for a reconceptualization of asceticism as a complex (viz. historical, modern and multicultural) phenomenon. Conversations are multi-disciplinary and respectful of a number of different sensibilities and religious and cultural traditions and agendas. Also, because the mini-conferences always have as their venue some address at which ascetic lifestyles and values are respected, often institutionalized, the Group has broadened and deepened its searching through conversations with hosts.

The Group has already learned the importance of accepting the diversity of practices and motives that is asceticism. This acceptance was the presupposition for the first project, a collection of texts exemplifying the broad range of ascetic motives, ideologies and practices in Greco-Roman and Christian Antiquity. Greek, Hebrew, Latin, Coptic and Syriac texts were collected, translated and put in (socio-political-historical) contexts (Wimbush). This project reflected not only the wide range of ascetic ideologies and practices, it also suggested the fruitfulness of a second project, the exploration of some of the different discursive formations in relation to different ascetic pieties in the period.

The fruitfulness of such a project is evident in its potential not only for clarifying particular issues and problems in particular texts or text-groups, but also as a heuristic key for the clearer understanding of the origins of and motives behind different religious self-definitions and orientations as they come into often obtuse, symbolic, histrionic, hyperbolic, even graphic literary expression. To know more about the language and rhetorical games that were played by author(s) of religious texts of antiquity, to be able to grasp the assumptions made, the rules observed in such games is to be in a more powerful hermeneutical position. To know more about how concern about the commendation of or opposition to certain asceticisms might be related to the playing of certain language and rhetorical games is even more significant: Asceticism provides focus upon a concrete phenomenon as topic that can be argued to be one of the most important for the understanding of religious sensibilities and religiously inspired orientations to society and culture—ancient and modern, east and west. As we have learned from Durkheim, van der Leeuw and other interpreters of religion, there can hardly be understanding of the polar extremes, or the very complicated in-between areas, of religious life and sensibilities without an understanding of the functions of ascetic piety and practices. Scholars of the history of Judaism and Christianity face an enormous corpus of literature that deals with asceticism; only fairly recently have a few among such scholars begun to address the intellectual, interpretive challenges of the universality of ascetic ideologies and practices. At any rate, the point is that the importance of asceticism cannot be overstated for any aspect of the critical study of religion—comparative, historical, phenomenological, philosophical, theological, literary.

As project, this collection of essays provides special opportunity for consideration of some important *methodological* challenges to the fields of study in which historical and philological and literary critical work interface, including intertestamental and biblical studies, patristics, church history. In general, it provides opportunity to further problematize the relationship between history and critical theory in religious studies. By providing a collection of essays that focus upon a concrete historical phenomenon (its great diversity notwithstanding) via certain types of critical (rhetorical, literary) questions (their diverse nuances notwithstanding), the volume is the more attractive and significant. It is an improvement over collections of essays that purport to highlight a particular method but encompass such a wide range of different topics that the application of the method leaves readers overwhelmed and confused, often unable to respond critically. It is also an improvement over those collections that focus on a single topic or phenomenon but nevertheless do not provide the sustained heuristic challenges and opportunities of a single line of exploration or method. Although the collection of essays that follows presents multi-authored arguments in consideration of a wide range of texts, all arguments are nonetheless focused upon the discursive, viz., rhetorical and literary, *arts* employed in efforts to commend or gainsay some type of ascetic piety. Pressing methodological challenges emerge from such interfacing and focus.

First, because the essays focus on a phenomenon that is arguably universal, they rightaway challenge that thinking and scholarship that continues to assume that asceticism can be pursued (with any degree of hermeneutical sophistication) strictly along tradition- or culture-specific lines (e.g. early Christian), or that it can be pursued within a particular tradition strictly according to historical period (e.g. Latin Christianity of the fourth and fifth centuries), region (e.g. Egypt or Syria), or literary genre (e.g. vitae) without recognition of the need for more generalizable and comparative categories of analysis. Because of the original constitution and focus of the Asceticism Group, most of the essays below fall within the single (but complex) tradition of early Christianity. Nevertheless, in their collective thrust or focus upon discursive formations and asceticisms the essays raise the question about the heuristic usefulness not only of the rubric "early Christianity," but also the traditional divisions (New Testament, Greek and Latin Christianity, Egyptian Christianity, and so forth) *within* the study of early Christianity, according to which their focus would normally be classified.

It is the topic of asceticism, its range and diversity, its complexity and historical and cultural persistence, its attractiveness and challenge to so many different fields and disciplines that first makes possible the appearance of such a range of essays with focus upon such different text-groups in one volume. Such a topic also inspires discussion across the standing divides in the study of religion—canonical and non-canonical, early and late, Greek and Latin, eastern and western, Jewish and Christian, Syriac and Egyptian, male and female, catholic and heretical, urban and rural, and so forth. Asceticism provides opportunity and challenge to redraw lines of inquiry and dialogue within the field of early Christianity and to engage other traditions on the basis of cross-disciplinary and cross-field conceptualization.

Second, because asceticism has to do with (meaningful) behavior, or practices, with certain types of understandings of and orientations to the world, and because it is a universal and complex phenomenon, coming to expression in many different literary, artistic and physical media, it should challenge all interpreters of religion to rethink methods and approaches and questions. Although it is true that social scientific and social historical studies have in recent years to a degree relativized the focus upon ideas and doctrines in scholarship in religion, it nonetheless is still the case that (too) much scholarship remains purely or merely idealist in focus. The challenge to find a topic, or a perspective, a paradigm, a theoretical framework that can facilitate a thoroughly historical, scientific, generalizable and comparative study of religion remains.

Asceticism is such a challenge. It provides at least the opportunity to shift focus in the study of religion toward a generalizable understanding of religion as meaningful or ideological praxis, as social-political orientation, as body language or signification. A complex theoretical framework that will facilitate understanding of such matters and, perhaps, provide something approaching a typology of asceticism is wanting.

Third, it is for obvious reasons especially important that such a framework include approaches to the study of the *literatures*, more broadly, the *discourses*, of times past. Focus on asceticism provides opportunity for interpreters of religion, especially those religious traditions strong on literary expressions, to address the challenges involved in choosing between or attempting to balance "history" and "literature," "history" and "critical theory" as primary approaches. Analyzing ancient religious texts primarily either as *sources* for explaining "what really happened," or as highly nuanced aesthetic representations should be seen as the naive divides they are (Cameron; Palmer). Asceticism, as meaningful behavior or praxis, forces consideration of both history and nuanced representation upon those who would understand its complexity.

Asceticism as focus of research presents the challenge of a topic that is, again, not only quite pervasive in the religious literatures of antiquity, it also has to do with history insofar as it has to do with behaviors, with orientations to the world. Thus, as focus of research it hardly sustains the separation of history and literature. It forces analysis of the origins and character of, and interaction between, macro-cultures and microcultures (viz. ascetic individuals and groups), thereby utilizing texts as certain types of socio-historical sources. It also makes use of the same texts in order to understand more about ancient religious aesthetics, mentalities, visions, rhetorical and literary representations, in sum, their discursive formations, "the structural features of symbolic forms which facilitate the mobilization of meaning" (Thompson: 292), "rules which determine what can and must be said from a certain position within social life . . . 'matri[ces] of meaning' . . ." (Eagleton: 195).

The ultimate opportunity that asceticism as focus of research provides, then, is the challenge to determine what might be the nature of the interrelationship of ascetic texts as historical sources and as discursive formations. Few topics provide as much opportunity for the problematizing and (re)conceptualizing of the critical study of religion.

Fourteen essays comprise the collection, divided in two parts: Part 1 is *Semeia* 57 and Part 2 is *Semeia* 58. Each is an attempt to understand how asceticism is part of the discursive strategies of the text or text-group under consideration. The collection does not purport to be the definitive application of discursive analysis, or the definitive study of asceticism. Nor would any of the essayists make the claim that his or her analysis of the respective text or text-group is comprehensive. The essays and their topics reflect the interest in, and differences in understanding of, both asceticism and discursive analysis on the part of a select number of scholars, not an attempt to cover all issues of concern. Nevertheless, the texts and topics included are, I want to argue, fairly diverse and quite interesting.

The essays are arranged on the basis of broad text-types—non-Christian, Greco-Roman; early Christian (New Testament, "fathers," "catholic," monastic). Within the categories identified no strict chronological order is followed, or is seen as necessary, given the focus of the collection.

1) Carol A. Newsom's "The Case of the Blinking I: Discourse of the Self at Qumram," inspired by the work of M. Foucault, is an exploration of the process by which Qumranites cultivated the self and discourse about the self, and developed a community discipline that included ascetic practices. By analyzing the Hodayot (Thanksgiving Hymns), Newsom seeks to account more precisely for the relationship between the particular type of discourse of cultivation of self discovered—"dynamically produced, non-unified, unstable subjectivity"—and the ascetic practices that were part of community discipline.

2) Leif E. Vaage's essay, "Like Dogs Barking: Cynic *Parrēsia* and Shameless Asceticism," is an examination of the "boldness of speech" of the Cynics as part of the discursive formation within which types of ascetic and other controversial practices are defended. Non-conventional speech and behavioral patterns are argued to be characteristic of an "asceticism of transgression."

3) "In Praise of Noble Women: Asceticism, Patronage and Honor" is the title of Karen J. Torjesen's contribution. It is an attempt to identify the literary and rhetorical strategy by which the traditional modes for honoring Roman male aristocrats were transferred to aristocratic female ascetics. The consequences of such a strategy, Torjesen argues, included the transcending of "the female personality."

4) Gail Paterson Corrington contributed the essay entitled "The Defense of the Body and the Discourse of Appetite: Continence and Control in the Greco-Roman World." It is an examination of the views of a wide

range of ancient Greek and Roman writers, including early Christian writers, regarding understandings of the complexity of the body, relationships between matter and soul/mind, and the discourses of control of the body for the cultivation of the self. Special attention is given to the challenges faced by women and the function of ascetic disciplines in the defining of the self "normally not accustomed to drawing its own boundaries."

5) Lucinda A. Brown's essay, "Asceticism and Ideology: The Language of Power in the Pastoral Epistles," probes the rhetoric and linguistic processes reflected in these second century New Testament documents, with a view to establishing how the general dominant ideological perspective was articulated and the structure of relationships, or power, was ordered in the communities behind the documents. The function of the discourse about a specific type of ascetic piety in the establishment of the structure of relationships in evidence in the documents is explained.

6) David G. Hunter, as the title of his essay "The Language of Desire: Clement of Alexandria's Transformation of Ascetic Discourse" suggests, explores the issue of the use of terminology for sexual desire and restraint in Clement's debate with so-called Gnostic and Encratite Christians. Hunter argues that Clement's strategy involved broadening the frame of reference for the debate, so as to suggest that there could be different types or facets of desire (*epithumia, orexis, hormē*), some of which could be embraced by all Christians. In the same vein, restraint (*enkrateia, sōphrosunē*) could also defined in broader terms, embracing a broader range of legitimate views and lifestyles.

7) "Allegory and Asceticism in Gregory of Nyssa" is Verna E. F. Harrison's examination of the relationship between the use of allegory in Scriptural interpretation and the pursuit of a type of ascetic discipline. Allegorical scriptural interpretation in the fourth–century Cappadocian church "father" Gregory, she argues, "mirror[s] ascetic behavior itself and conversely embodies a redirection of human drives and activities."

8) Neal Kelsey's essay, "The Body as Desert in *The Life of St. Anthony*," argues that the narrative document about the third/fourth–century Egyptian desert hermit offers a "topographical map" of a fictive desert. The features of such a map—the spatial metaphors—are said to spring from the basic experiences of a type of corporeality in which mind-body dualism is respected and justified. The body, of course, is viewed negatively, corresponding to the narrative map that is desert. In the same way that the narrative desert is to be overcome, just so the human body must be overcome. Thus, ascetic practices are commended through a myth of origins for a movement ascribing Anthony as founding figure.

9) Marilyn Nagy's "Translocation of Parental Images in Fourth-Century Ascetic Texts: Motifs and Techniques of Identity" is an application of object relations theory and anthropology to the critical reading of selected fourth-century texts about Anthony, Pachomius, Theodore and Ammon. She reads in the texts attempts on the part of these ascetics to realize a counter-cultural identity by reflecting aspects of the ideals of their culture.

10) Emphasis on Egyptian monasticism continues with James E. Goehring's essay entitled "Through A Glass Darkly: Diverse Images of the *APOTAKTIKOI(AI)* Of Early Egyptian Monasticism." The essay focuses on the problem created by the increasing papyrological evidence supporting *apotaktikos* as preferred term of reference for Egyptian ascetics. The problem is heightened because often the term is inclusive of the two traditional exclusive categories for the Egyptian ascetic—the anchoritic and coenobitic ascetic. Goehring argues that the problem lies in too much dependence upon *literary* sources that created, and perhaps needed to sustain, the division. His argument provides impetus for his (and others') careful study of the origins and (socio-political) functions of the categories by which ascetic lifestyles and *virtuosi* are labeled, and the wider discursive strategies to which such terms belong.

11) In his essay, "Demons and the Perfecting of the Monk's Body: Monastic Anthropology, Daemonology, and Asceticism," Richard Valantasis draws attention to the role of "daemons" in monastic literature. In the latter the formation of the monk and progress in the monastic life depend upon success in the constant warfare against "daemons." Thus, the appearance of "daemons" in the literature helps establish asceticism (*askēsis*) as a metaphor, a term taken from the world of the athlete to explain a basic aspect of the religious life. Valantasis argues that "monk" and "daemons" were also understood along the same lines, the former pointing to a rather complex "re-location" of the body relative to God and the angels by means of social withdrawal and isolation, the latter, as personifications of human experience, pointing to the body's desires and resistance to the cultivation of virtue.

12) Vincent L. Wimbush contributed the essay entitled "Ascetic Piety and Color-ful Language: Stories About Ethiopian Moses." It is an exploration of the use of the language of color differences in the narratives about the Black Ethiopian monk named Moses. An attempt is made to establish the relationships between the radical opposites of racial color differences (the blackness of Moses, on the one hand, and the non-blackness of others, on the other), and the radical opposites in orientation to the world (the monastic life, on the one hand, and the non-monastic existence, on the other), in some narratives assumed, in other narratives

established. The discursive fields or strategies that can be assumed to be behind the language games played in the narratives are discussed.

13) Virginia Burrus authored "Ascesis, Authority and Text: *The Acts of the Council of Saragossa*" as a case study exploration of the interrelationship between the contours of debates about ascetic practices and the contours of exercise of episcopal authority. A broadening of the concept of asceticism, as well as the genres reflective of ascetic pieties, is urged.

14) Jason BeDuhn in a provocative essay entitled "A Regimen for Salvation: Medical Models in Manichaean Asceticism" argues that the highly graphic medical language and language of renunciation of Manichaean literature were intended to be apprehended as literally as they were graphic. With respect to Manichaean literature in particular, and by logical extension to other religious literature, he therefore cautions against the general bent toward metaphorizing and spiritualizing interpretations.

Geoffrey Harpham, professor of English, Tulane University, author of the well received book *The Ascetic Imperative in Culture and Criticism* (1987), offers a critical response to the essays, focusing on some essays as a springboard for the broadening and deepening of critical discussion about asceticism beyond early Christian and Greco-Roman texts and issues to modern and postmodern cultural expressions and sensibilities. Harpham's argument that renunciation is not new, but is resurgent as cultural expression that now takes on different forms and meanings beyond strictly religious traditions, is provocative and leaves the door open for exchange with him and others across disciplines and fields, traditions and sensibilities.

To the chagrin of James Goehring (if I have read his essay with understanding!), but for the edification of the reader, a glossary of technical terms used in many of the essays is appended.

A special word of gratitude is due to my friends and colleagues Leif Vaage and Richard Valantasis for their encouragement and advice, and thorough and critical reading of essays here included.

WORKS CONSULTED

Cameron, Averil
    1990   *Christianity and the Rhetoric of Empire: The Development of Christian Discourse*. Berkeley: University of California Press.

Palmer, Bryan D.
  1990   *Descent into Discourse: The Reification of Language and the Writing of Social History.* Philadelphia: Temple University Press.

Eagleton, Terry
  1991   *Ideology: An Introduction.* London: Verso.

Thompson, John B.
  1990   *Ideology and Modern Culture: Critical Social Theory in the Era of Mass Communication.* Stanford: Stanford University Press.

Wimbush, Vincent L., ed.
  1990   *Ascetic Behavior in Greco-Roman Antiquity: A Sourcebook.* Minneapolis: Fortress.

I

THE CASE OF THE BLINKING I:
DISCOURSE OF THE SELF AT QUMRAN

Carol A. Newsom
Candler School of Theology
Emory University

ABSTRACT

Michel Foucault once posed the question, "What must one know about oneself in order to be willing to renounce anything?" Since the Qumran community required its members to submit to a rigorous discipline, it is worth asking how the community developed a discourse of the self and how that discourse of the self was related to the community's life of discipline. The Hodayot or Thanksgiving Hymns from Qumran provide a particularly good context within which to pose such questions.

Introduction

In an article completed shortly before his death Michel Foucault raised the issue of what he called "Technologies of the Self." As Foucault put it: "Max Weber posed the question: If one wants to behave rationally and regulate one's actions according to true principles, what part of one's self should one renounce? What is the ascetic price of reason? . . . . I posed the opposite question: How have certain kinds of interdictions required the price of certain kinds of knowledge about oneself? What must one know about oneself in order to be willing to renounce anything?" (17).[1] It is an interesting question to pose in relation to the Qumran community. The person who entered the covenant of the community agreed to renounce a great deal. He swore to submit to the authority of the community in matters of *halakah*. His relations with persons outside the group were severely restricted. His own property was turned over to the community. Various behaviors, including gestures, the arrangement of garments, and even bodily functions were subject to regulation. It was not only non-verbal behaviors but also practices of speech that were disciplined at Qumran. The sectarian was required to undergo periodic examinations in which he gave an account of his conduct and opinions, a procedure that determined his status within the community. It is the regulation of speech in particular that I want to take as the starting point for an examination of the discourse of the self at Qumran.

The Disciplines of Speech and the Discourse of the Self

Not fortuitously did the sect designate itself as עצת היחד, "the counsel/council of the community." It was fundamentally a group of persons seeking to be conformed to the "counsel of God" (1QS 1:8) through a form of life that had at its center the act of taking counsel together. An individual's knowledge and speech, no less than his wealth, became the property of the community, to be disciplined and exercised for the communal benefit (1QS 1:11–13; 6:22–23). The extended account of a "session of the many" in column 6 of the Serek ha-Yahad gives a sense of the discipline of taking counsel together as practiced at Qumran.

> This is the rule for a session of the many. Each (shall sit) according to his rank.... In the same order they shall be asked for judgement, or concerning any counsel or matter which has to do with the many, each man offering his knowledge to the council of the community. No man shall interrupt his neighbour's words before his brother has finished speaking, or speak before one registered in rank before him. A man who is asked shall speak in his turn. In a session of the many no man shall say anything which is not approved by the many and, indeed, by the overseer of the many. Any man who has something to say to the many, but is not entitled to question the council of the community, shall stand on his feet and say, 'I have something to say to the many.' If they tell him to speak, he shall speak (1QS 6.8–13; trans. Knibb).[2]

This disciplined exercise of speech reflects an ambivalence about the individual voice. It is, on the one hand, essential to the production of knowledge of the will of God. But its autonomy is thoroughly hedged about with the protocols of rank, etiquette, and consensus. What did a sectarian have to know about himself in order for this discipline of speech to seem meaningful, even self-evidently correct and appropriate? To a significant extent the texts from Qumran known as the Thanksgiving Hymns or Hodayot are devoted to the construction of a discourse of the self.[3] It should prove possible to discover in these texts something about the relationship between knowledge of the self and the discipline of the community, especially the discipline of speech.

First person speech, such as one finds in the Hodayot, has an especially direct relationship to the constitution of subjectivity, since the pronoun "I" does not refer to a concept, as most words do, but has meaning only in concrete situations of discourse, as speakers appropriate the pronoun and define themselves within discourse (Benveniste: 226–27). The Hodayot, of course, are not generally thought to be spontaneous acts of speech but literary prayers. The first person style, however, facilitates the identification of the reader or hearer with the subjectivity constructed in the text because it blurs the distinction between the speaking subject who actually produces the speech, the subject of speech produced within the discourse, and the spoken subject who "agrees" to be signified by the discourse (see Silverman: 198).

In the Hodayot one of the most pervasive themes is that of knowledge. Repeatedly, the subject in the Hodayot associates itself with knowledge and indeed constitutes itself as a subject of knowledge, as one who knows. See, for example, the *hodayah* in col. 15:

> "And I know, by means of the understanding that comes from you, that it is not through the power of flesh [that an individual may be righteous, nor] does one's own conduct belong to a person, nor is humankind able to direct its steps. And I know that the inclination of every spirit is in your hand, [and all] its [activi]ty you established before you created it" (1QH 15:12–14).

This knowing voice, which repeatedly says "I know . . . I know" and which has grasped the principle of the divine ordering of human existence is, upon closer examination, rather elusive. The knowledge through which it speaks is not its own but God's ("I know, by means of the understanding that comes from you . . . "). It is this gift of knowledge that in a very real sense brings the speaker into being as a subject. And it is in the act of recitation of such knowledge that the subject grasps himself as in a sense newly created by God as one who knows.

The self is thus constituted in the Hodayot as a subject of knowledge. But the self of the Hodayot is not only a subject of knowledge but an object of knowledge as well. The voice that speaks may also direct attention to, make judgments on, and even recoil in horror from, its "own self." The self of the Hodayot is both the knower and the known, the observing and observed self. What one discovers is a curious bifurcation of subjectivity, which is enacted over and over again in numerous *hodayot*. The moment of crisis, in which the self is experienced as divided, is often presented as a crisis in knowledge or a crisis in speech (e.g. 1QH 1, 10, 12, 13). The recognition of the observed self throws into question the knowledge and discourse that is constitutive of the observing self. The work of the Hodayot is to validate its knowledge and speech in the face of that dismaying recognition.

The *hodayah* in 1QH 13:1–21 provides a good example of this dynamic. The composition has been recently reconstructed by Puech as a hodayah of the *maskil* (1988a).[4] Knowledge of the mysteries of God is a prominent theme, with strong echoes of the "Two Spirits" section of 1QS 3–4. The crisis comes as the knowing, observing self turns its knowing gaze on itself. The self it discovers is described in highly negative terms. It is so far from the moral agency presupposed in biblical narrative, law, and wisdom traditions, that it is hardly recognizable from biblical perspective as a "self" at all. "But ho[w i]s a spirit of flesh to discern all these things and to grasp the secret counsel of great [. . .]? And what is one born of woman amid all your fearful works? He is a thing constructed of dust and kneaded with water. [Sin]ful gui[lt] is his foundation, ignominious shame, and a source of pollution. And a spirit of error rules him. And if he acts wickedly, he will become [a sign] forever and an emblem for generations, an eternal horror among flesh" (1QH 13:13–16 = Puech 5:30–33). Here is a being without capacity for knowledge or moral judgment and action. Described in terms of dust and water, it lacks the animating breath of God that distinguishes a living being from inert stuff (see Gen. 2:7). The "spirit" that does characterize it is either the wonderfully oxymoronic "spirit of flesh" or the "spirit of error" that indicates its inability to direct itself properly. No wonder that it is an object of loathing and horror to the voice that contemplates it. This is the language of genuine masochism.[5] Here the self enacts its own nothingness in radical contrast to the being of God. To its pollution corresponds the holiness of God; to its guilt, God's righteousness; to its inability to will and to do, God's uniquely autonomous will and creative power; to its lowliness among the works of God, God's own absolute incomparability. The matter of the relationship between the observed and observing self is perplexing. It is a question that would never occur to one to raise in connection with the Psalms. There the self may be suffering and guilty, but its speaking voice seems wholly unified with its experience. Indeed the quality of that voice is generated out of the suffering and guilt it experiences.[6] In the Hodayot, however, the observed self does not appear as a being capable of the self-reflectiveness or the subtle consciousness that we encounter in the speaking voice of the prayer. Indeed it does not and cannot generate the voice that says "I know." The understanding, the *binah* that constitutes that voice, is *binatka*, God's *binah*. Its understanding is a gift, not a given.

Where, then, is the self of the Hodayot? On the one hand, as one tries to trace out the self observed and described, it vanishes into a masochistic nullity. But if one tries to trace out the self that observes and speaks, it, too, elusively vanishes back into God. The subject constituted by the Hodayot is neither the one nor the other but is dynamically produced as the uneasy intersection of the two. It is an unstable construction that defies representation as a unitary consciousness. I certainly would not want to say that the authors of the Hodayot were proto-postmodern deconstructionists, but what is produced in the Hodayot is a type of what the postmodernists would call a "decentered self." In a way that is far more radical than what one finds in the Psalms the initial impression of the speaking subject as a coherent source of experience, meaning, and expression is progressively dismantled. Knowledge and discourse are finally validated, not by the reconstitution of a unified self but precisely by the sacrifice of such a self. One could trace this process in the lines following the section quoted above (see 1QH 13.16–23 = Puech 5.33–40), but the dynamic is more clearly preserved in the *hodayah* contained in 1QH 1. This text also provides an opportunity to see how certain other aspects of sectarian subjectivity are developed.

The beginning of the composition is unfortunately not preserved but probably occurred near the top of the column (Puech 1988b:52). As the text becomes legible, it is clear that the topic is praise of God. In an act of praise the speaker constructs the object of praise by the qualities selected for attention and by the traditions and style of language used. But the speaker also constructs a character for himself or herself. The selection of language and traditions will reveal something of what sort of person speaks. The speaker will also construct his or her subject position by the stance taken with respect to the object of praise: whether the speaker shares or lacks the qualities of the one praised; what motivates the praise; whether the speaker's action of praising is effaced or made a focus of attention; how the act of praise affects the one who utters it; what meaning it has for the one who speaks it, etc.

In the passage in question the qualities of God initially praised are various: power, counsel, jealousy (but also patient judgment), and righteousness. But in line 7 a long section (lines 7–20) begins in which the wisdom of God in creation is explored in detail.[7] The qualities of divine creativity are expressed in a way familiar from other Qumran texts. What is celebrated is the ability to intend, to plan, to do. No activity stands outside the divine plan. Everything that happens is simply the making visible of the divine plan in which everything was already known. And indeed what marks the created world as the expression of the divine plan is its obedient and rule–ordered activity. The vocabulary of order is extensive: standard, rules, domains, paths, task, service, purposes, and mysteries (which are esoteric purposes). Creator and creation are symmetrically arranged. Autonomy marks the one; heteronomy the other.

Almost any text can be said to articulate a pattern of desire, a phenomenon of readers' experience discussed by Booth (201–24). Texts of praise are especially active in this kind of work, since an object of praise is an object of desire. But just as some desires are stimulated through the text, others are prohibited and must be repressed. The text of 1QH 1 does not inspire in its readers the desire for autonomy: to intend, to plan, and to do. That belongs to God. To desire it would be blasphemy. The desire for autonomy is implicitly put under the sign of prohibition. Instead, the desire the text stimulates is the desire to discover oneself as ordered, as ruled, as known from of old, a subject whose destiny was always intended. It is that recognition that draws one close to the plan of God and thus to the object of all desire.

The passage would not be so persuasive if it merely stated its values. The reader is persuaded that he already is "that kind of desirer" because the voice that speaks enacts its subjectivity. The act of praise that runs from line 7 through line 20 is a beautifully ordered discourse. It is contained within an *inclusio* that praises God's primordial wisdom and foreknowledge in closely similar expressions (lines 7–9 and 18–20). In between it maps the cosmos: the heavens (lines 9–13), the earth and the seas (lines 13–15), and the human realm (lines 15–18). The syntax, even though it is difficult to decipher in places, clearly makes use of elaborate parallel structures, especially in lines 11–13. The vocabulary, as noted earlier, is replete with expressions for ordered obedience. Only one who has already been shaped by a desire to be "set in order according to your will" (line 15) can speak like this.

But there is something else one needs to notice about the voice that speaks. What kind of voice can speak so clearly about the divine will and plan, about the mysteries of the heavens, the orderly structures of the cosmos, and even about events of future judgment? The character that it creates for itself is quintessentially a character of knowledge and of intimacy with the sorts of knowledge that are the provenance of God. In fact, it is just at the conclusion of this act of praise that the speaker steps outside the frame, so to speak, to comment on what makes possible his act of praise and what it is that constitutes him as a subject of knowledge: "These things I know because of the insight that comes from you, for you have opened my ears to wondrous mysteries" (line 21).

Yet immediately upon uttering these words, the subject that has spoken so sublimely seems plunged into crisis as it contemplates itself. The language of masochism is unleashed as the self repudiates itself in disgust. It is described in terms that are the inverse of the divine autonomous will, wisdom, and righteousness. It is a creature of inert clay and water, without understanding, both unclean and guilty. The result of this self-disclosure is to call into question the meaning and value of the author's speech. "What could I say that is not already known, or what could I declare that has not already been told? Everything is engraved before you in an inscription of record for all the everlasting times, and the cycles of the number of the everlasting years with all their appointed times. They are not hidden nor missing from your presence" (lines 23–25). It is a curious passage. Coming as it does immediately after the masochistic self-encounter, it is apparently a denigration of the speech of the speaker. He can offer nothing new, nothing not already possessed. The emptiness, the nullity of the self is experienced even in the performance of praise, an act that had seemed to place the speaker in a privileged, powerful position. It is noteworthy that the confession of personal lack merges almost imperceptibly into a confession of divine fullness. The resolution to the crisis of subjectivity and speech lies in that dynamic. But the prayer is not yet ready to move toward resolution. The composition turns again to the inadequacies of speech. Just as his speech about God was felt to be inadequate, so he finds it impossible to speak in defense of himself in the presence of God: "And how should a person explain his sin, and how should he defend his iniquities? And how should he reply to every righteous judgment? To you, O you God of knowledge, belong all works of righteousness and the counsel of truth. But to mortal beings belongs the service of iniquity and the works of deceit" (lines 25–27). The two elements of this double crisis are apparently related, since the prayer suggests elsewhere that moral cleanness is necessary for one who would praise God (lines 32–33). Thus the recognition of the speaker's sinful condition renders his act of praise deeply problematic.

The resolution to this crisis of speech is achieved by pursuing the logic of masochistic subjectivity to its conclusion. Even speech, traditionally that most intimate expression of self (Fisch:107–8), derives not from some autonomous self but from God: "You created breath for the tongue, you know its words, and you establish the fruit of the lips before they exist. You set the words to verse, and the utterance of the breath of the lips by measure. And you bring forth the lines according to their mysteries and the utterances of the breath according to their design, in order to make known your glory and to recount your wonders through all your deeds of truth and the j[ud]gm[ent]s of your [ri]ghteousness, and to praise your name with every mouth" (lines 27–31). There is some question whether lines 28–29 use technical terminology for poetic speech, as my translation suggests. Whether or not they do, the important thing is that the speaker's speech is recognized as being ordered, ruled, subject to design, just like the phenomena of the cosmos described in the earlier part of the composition. Only as the speaker gives up any claim of autonomous speech does his discourse receive value. He has standing to speak, not because he can demonstrate his righteousness, but because "you have cleansed [me] from great iniquity in order to recount your wonders before all your creatures.... all your wonders by which you have shown yourself strong [through me....]" (lines 32–33). The poem concludes, then, with the enactment of this newly empowered speech in an address in the bold wisdom style: "Hear, O you sages, and you who ponder knowledge ... " (line 35).

This composition is quite a *tour de force* for the construction of the subject position of the reader. It begins with a beautifully crafted act of praise that implies a speaker of powerful knowledge. Yet at the same time it discourages the desire for autonomy and offers as desirable an existence that is measured, governed, and subjected by the divine autonomy. The positive lure to the embrace of such a subjectivity is reinforced by staging a crisis for the self and its speech. If its speech is grounded in itself, then such speech is valueless, for the individual is utterly vile. Only by recognizing that nothing comes from the self, that there is no autonomous self, can one receive back the speech that unites the speaker with the object of its desire and so empowers it. What the prayer enacts is an evacuation of the self and a reconstruction of it as an effect of God. Discourse and the self are secured only through the dynamic experience of negation.

Conclusions

To return then to Foucault's question—"How have certain kinds of interdictions required the price of certain kinds of knowledge about oneself? What must one know about oneself in order to be willing to renounce anything?" The patterns of subjectivity that are established through *hodayot* such as the ones examined here constitute the experience and knowledge of the self required by the disciplines of the Qumran community, especially the disciplines of speech. This is not to make causal claims or functionalist ones but only to recognize that selves and communities are mutually produced through discourse and stand as emblems of one another (Brown:19).

Several of these correspondences are worth noting. The persona of the Hodayot is one who is constituted through the act of speech, the act of telling what he knows. The cultivation of individuals whose sense of self was deeply connected with the act of speech was important because of the centrality of discourse in the life of the community. The periodic examinations of the members of the community concerning their "insight" and "deeds" required individuals for whom giving an account of themselves was a meaningful act, though the modes of speech would have differed in prayer and in examination. Taking counsel together in a session of the many required one to speak out in the presence of one's superiors. A self formed by the language of the Hodayot has the ability to speak in that way because he knows himself to have been granted insight by God.

But the act of taking counsel together also required restraint and submission of the individual voice to the protocols of the many. The Hodayot cultivate a subject for whom authority to speak is naturally paired with discipline. The knowledge for which the psalmist gives thanks is not something that could be grasped as an individual possession. The reception of it is inseparable from the giving up of claims to autonomy, inseparable from a desire to be subjected to the ruled and ordered structures of

God's will. And so the various prohibitions that hedged about his speech and conduct would have been experienced as part of this order.

In other respects, too, the formation of the subject in the Hodayot serves the disciplines of the community. The desire to be conformed to the will of God was not unproblematic. Members of the community were required to practice mutual reproof, both in private and before witnesses. Catalogues of rules and punishments also imply the use of sanctions. The willingness of members to submit to the judgment of the community would have been enhanced by the self-confrontation practiced in the Hodayot, in which the enlightened, knowing aspect of the subject confronts its persistently recalcitrant aspect, its susceptibility to a "spirit of error."

In general, the complex ethos of the community required a distinctive subjectivity in which aspects of both assertion and submissiveness were cultivated. The individual speaking subject was essential for the central value of taking counsel together but also a potential threat to the hierarchical, collective organization of the sect. The discourse of the self in the Hodayot with its dynamically produced, non-unified, unstable subjectivity—what I have jocularly called the "blinking I"—represents one of the most significant ways in which such a self was produced at Qumran.

NOTES

[1] It is not my intent to pursue a self-consciously Foucauldian inquiry in this paper, but I find Foucault's inversion of the question provocative.

[2] Unless otherwise noted all translations are my own.

[3] For purposes of this paper I am excluding from consideration those Hodayot often associated with the Righteous Teacher.

[4] The reconstruction by Puech joins fragments 15a, 17, 20, 31, and 33 to the text of col. 13. The translation is based on Puech's improved readings.

[5] I am using the term "masochism" here in a manner similar to that of Peter Berger. It is "an intensification of this self-denying surrender to society and its order . . . the attitude in which the individual reduces himself to an inert and thinglike object. . . . Its key characteristic is the intoxication of surrender to an other—complete, self-denying, even self-destroying. . . . 'I am nothing—He is everything—and therein lies my ultimate bliss'—in this formula lies the essence of the masochistic attitude" (55–56).

[6] The construction of the subject in the Psalms is also a complex phenomenon. The subject in the Psalms has its own instabilities, but they are different from those of the Hodayot. See Harold Fisch. The dynamics of the presentation of the self in psalms of lament and thanksgiving is explored by Thorkild Jacobsen.

[7] "In your wisdom [you] es[tablished the generations of] eternity, and before you created them, you knew their deeds for everlasting ages. [For without you nothing] is done. And nothing is known without your will. You formed every spirit, and [. . .] and the standard for all their deeds. And you stretched out the heavens for your glory, all [. . .] you [. . .] according to your will, and strong winds according to their rules. Before they came to be ho[ly] messengers [. . .] to the eternal spirits in their dominions: luminaries according to their mysteries, stars according to the[ir] paths, [. . .]

according to their task, flashes and lightning according to their service, and the treasuries devised for th[eir] purposes [. . .] according to their mysteries. You created the earth through your strength, the seas and the deeps [. . . and all] their [inhabi]tants you established through your wisdom, and all that is in them you set in order according to your will [. . .] to the human spirit that you fashioned in the world for all the days of eternity and everlasting generations to [. . .] in their times. You allotted their service throughout all their generations and the jud[gm]ent in the times appointed for them according to the domi[nion. . .] their [. . .] for every generation, and a visitation for their well-being together with all their afflictions [. . .] And you allotted it to all their offspring according to the number of the generations of eternity and for all the everlasting years [. . .] And in the wisdom of your knowledge you established their destiny before they existed. According to [your will] everything [comes] into being; and without you nothing is done" (1QH 7–20).

WORKS CONSULTED

Benveniste, Emile.
    1971   *Problems in General Linguistics.* Trans. Mary Elizabeth Meek. Coral Gables: University of Miami Press.

Berger, Peter
    1969   *The Sacred Canopy.* Garden City, NY: Doubleday.

Booth, Wayne
    1988   *The Company We Keep.* Chicago: University of Chicago Press.

Brown, Richard Harvey
    1987   "Personal Identity and Political Economy: Western Grammars of the Self in Historical Perspective." Pp. 28–63 in *Society as Text.* Chicago: University of Chicago Press.

Fisch, Harold
    1987   "Psalm: The Limits of Subjectivity." Pp. 104–35 in *Poetry with a Purpose.* Bloomington: Indiana University Press.

Foucault, Michel
    1988   "Technologies of the Self." Pp. 16–49 in *Technologies of the Self: A Seminar with Michel Foucault.* Ed. Luther H. Martin, Huck Gutman, and Patrick H. Hutton. London: Travistock.

Jacobsen, Thorkild
    1976   "Personal Religion." Pp. 147–64 in *The Treasures of Darkness.* New Haven: Yale University Press.

Knibb, Michael A.
  1987   *The Qumran Community*. Cambridge Commentaries on Writings of the Jewish & Christian World 200 BC to AD 200, vol. 2. Cambridge: Cambridge University Press.

Puech, Emile
  1988a   "Un hymne essénien en partie retrouvé et les béatitudes." *RevQ* 49–52:59–88.
  1988b   "Quelque aspects de la restauration du Rouleau des Hymnes (1QH)." *JJS* 39:38–55.

Silverman, Kaja
  1983   *The Subject of Semiotics*. New York. Oxford University Press.

LIKE DOGS BARKING:
CYNIC *PARRĒSIA* AND SHAMELESS ASCETICISM

Leif E. Vaage
Emmanuel College
University of Toronto

ABSTRACT

Cynic *parrēsia* or "boldness of speech" is best understood as the discursive formation which articulated the "shameless" ascetic practice of the ancient "dog-philosophers." Evidence of both Cynic *parrēsia* and their "shamelessness," as well as how the different components of each related to one another, is presented in this essay. The suggestion is made that we view both the habits of speech and personal comportment by the Cynics as basic features of an "asceticism of transgression."

0. Introduction

By the term "discursive formation" something subtler with greater institutional power lurking in its referential folds is usually meant than the mouthy impudence typically associated with the Cynic virtue of *parrēsia* = "boldness of speech." It is, moreover, extremely difficult to pin anything like the term "formation" on the Cynics. In antiquity the idea of Cynic "theory" could hardly be maintained. Nonetheless, for the better part of 1000 years from classical Athens to Christian Rome, one knew when a member of the "breed" (versus someone else) was hounding.

From the point of view of "serious" thought, ancient Cynicism is extremely weak on important concepts and definitions. This is what late nineteenth-century classical historians meant when they referred to the Cynics as "popular" philosophers. As Diogenes Laertius notes at the end of his account of them in *Lives of Eminent Philosophers* (6.103), some maintained that the Cynics represented "just a way of life" (*enstasis biou*), instead of being "really a philosophy" (*hairēsin kai tautēn . . . tēn philosophian*).

Even Cynic claims to be "following nature" are dramatically short of systemic range and rigor. The concept "following nature," in the mouth of the Cynics, amounted to little more than a summary of ad hoc analogies in defense of their questionable behavior (see, e.g., Pseudo-Diogenes 6, 16,

36, 42; Diogenes Laertius 6.22, 23, 38; Pesudo-Lucian, *The Cynic* 15; Julian 6.193d). There is nothing in the literature of Cynicism at all comparable to the definition of "nature" given in Diogenes Laertius' account of Stoicism (7.148–49), or the one developed earlier by Aristotle.

Neither the chreia nor the diatribe, both literary genres long linked to Cynicism, can be said to have originated with it (Hock/O'Neil:3–7; Kindstrand:97–99). Likewise, the use of these styles of speech was never the privileged or exclusive domain of the Cynics. It is true that much of what we know about the Cynics has come down to us in these forms. But this fact alone does not provide us with a sufficiently strong basis on which to make any meaningful judgment about the relationship between Cynic discourse and ascetic practice.

To compound matters further, some may question whether the Cynics even had an ascetic practice (though such a question should be examined in its own right to explore the relationship between our own discourse about ancient asceticism and the social practices that these post/modern distinctions manage.) The Cynics' claim, for example, that their way of life was a "short cut to happiness" or virtue (see, e.g., Pseduo-Crates 6, 13, 16, 21; Pseudo-Diogenes 12, 30, 44; Julian 7.225c; Diogenes Laertius 6.38–39, 104) is hardly of a piece with the long drawn-out labors of asceticism characteristic of Syrian holy men in the fifth and six centuries CE. And what about all those stories of Cynics who regularly overindulged in food, masturbated in public, and carried on sexually in other ways that reveal not the slightest concern for bodily control? This is not asceticism as we have been taught to imagine it!

I assume, nonetheless, that the repeatedly cited Cynic virtue of *parrēsia* was indeed a kind of discursive formation and that the Cynics were, furthermore, shameless ascetics. I will present evidence for both of these assumptions and suggest at the same time how the different components of each relate to one another. An opportunity is provided by such a review to reconsider typical characterizations of Cynic discourse and behavior, as well as further to extend and specify the meaning of asceticism as a form of cultural activity in Greco-Roman antiquity.

1. *Cynic Discourse as parrēsia*

We begin with some examples of Cynic *parrēsia*. That this discursive style was typical of the Cynics is clear, if only because of Epictetus' (3.22.19, 93if) and Julian's (6.201a) uneasy efforts while idealizing Cynicism to restrict who could avail themselves of such an interlocutory manner. "Being asked what was the most beautiful thing in the world, [Diogenes] replied: *parrēsia*" (Diogenes Laertius 6.69).

The quintessential example of Cynic *parrēsia* is perhaps the much rehearsed account of a conversation between Alexander the Great and Diogenes of Sinope. Predictably, what was said between the two varies from version to version:

> Alexander once came and stood opposite him and said, "I am Alexander the great king." "And I," said he, "am Diogenes the dog" (Diogenes Laertius 6.60; cf. 6.63).

> When Alexander stood opposite him and asked, "Are you not afraid of me?" "Why, what are you?" said he, "a good thing or a bad?" When Alexander replied, "A good thing," "Who then," said Diogenes, "is afraid of the good?" (Diogenes Laertius 6.68).

> When Alexander asked him to name anything he wanted, "Just now," [Diogenes] said, "stand a bit away from the sun" (Cicero, *Tusc. Disp.* 5.32; see also Diogenes Laertius 6.38; Dio Chrysostom 4.14).

> I was seated in the theater gluing together pages of a book, when Alexander, the son of Philip, came up and stood directly opposite near me, and blocked my sunlight. I looked up, because I could no longer see the joins of the pages at all, and recognized him at my side. When he also recognized me as I looked up, he greeted me and offered me his right hand. And so I greeted him in return and spoke to this effect. "You are truly invincible, my boy, since you are capable of the same things as the gods. For look, they say of the moon, that it disposes of the sun by getting in its way, and you have done the same thing by coming here and standing near me."
> Then Alexander said, "Diogenes, you are joking."
> "What do you mean?" I retorted. "First of all, can't you see that I am kept from my work because I can't see, as though it were night. And secondly, although it means nothing to me to be discussing these things with you now, I am in fact doing so."
> "Nothing?" he said. "Is that how much Alexander the king matters to you?"
> "Not even a little," I said. . . .
> While I was expounding on all these points with great inspiration, a great sense of awe came over Alexander and, leaning toward one of his companions, he said, "Had I not been born Alexander first, I would have been Diogenes." And making me rise, he tried to lead me away with him, urging me to campaign with him. But reluctantly he let me go (Pseudo–Diogenes 33; cf. Juvenal, *Satires* 14.311–14; Diogenes Laertius 6.32).

"Boldness of speech" describes here what exasperated parents are wont to call an "attitude problem." It is not so much what is said as *how* it is said, and *to whom* it matters.

Cynic *parrēsia* was distinguished less by its specific content and more by its relation to the socio-rhetorical situation in which a given statement was uttered. In the mouth of a Cynic, *parrēsia* meant saying whatever whenever wherever in such a way as to provoke the consistent sensation of "boldness." Diogenes of Sinope, the Cynic par excellence, tosses back at Alexander the Great the quintessential conqueror's formidable achievements (cf. Julian, 7.212cd). Unimpressed by the general's right to be accorded respect and awe, the philosopher's response leaves no doubt as to the Cynic's basic indifference, if not diffidence, toward every such symbol of cultural prestige.

What lies behind such studied impudence? In part, an impudent unstudiedness. Cynic *parrēsia* was not the consequence of expertise in a field of ancient arts and sciences, demonstrated by the consequent ability to speak with skill and rhetorical flourish; it was instead the reflection of refusing to learn anything that formed part of the ordinary subjects of instruction. If Diogenes Laertius can be believed, the Cynics did away with logic and physics (*ton physikon topon*)—though they otherwise claimed to be "following nature" (*physis*)—along with geometry and music and all such things: "At least Antisthenes used to say that those who had attained discretion had better not study literature, lest they should be perverted by alien influences" (Diogenes Laertius 6.103–104). A more positive rationale is suggested in one of the Cynic epistles:

> Your pupil Euremus offered me captious arguments and riddles with as much embellishment as he was capable of. But I do not think that virtue is dignified by such talk, which is like decorative boxes that are empty and hard to open, but rather by a style of life which can properly be shown naked to those who chance upon it (Pseudo-Diogenes 50).

Cynic discourse as *parrēsia* opposed the "refined" speech of the educated. The Cynics spoke "street" Greek. To what extent they controlled this style of utterance and to what extent they had no choice but to speak as they did, given their rejection of "proper" rhetorical training, is impossible to determine. There is an amusing anecdote told by Philostratus in *The Lives of the Sophists* about Peregrinus Proteus, an infamous Cynic of the second century CE. Peregrinus is said to have hounded Herodes, constantly harrassing him "in a semi-barbarous tongue" (*en hēmibarbaro glottē*) until, one day, Herodes felt compelled to reply: "Granted that you must malign me, but do you have to do it with such bad language?" (Philostratus 2.1; LCL, p. 176). Likewise, Dio Chrysostom in his thirty-second discourse to the people of Alexandria, seeking to distinguish himself from the Cynics, "of which there is no small crowd in this city," refers to those that positioned themselves "at street corners, in alleyways, and at temple gates" who "string together rough jokes and much tittle-tattle and that low badinage that smacks of the marketplace" (32.9).

From one point of view, therefore, Cynic *parrēsia* was simply tasteless talk. From another perspective, however, it came highly spiced, both with wit and with denunciatory verve. Both of these elements are key ingredients of Cynic *parrēsia*. We would be in error if we assumed that Cynic "boldness of speech" meant simply a relentless haranguing of one's audience without a corresponding sense of humor, or vice versa. In fact, it was precisely the fact that one could never be sure exactly what would come out of a Cynic's mouth that helped to make their reputation for *parrēsia*.

Harshness of speech was regularly attributed to the Cynics in offhanded characterizations like the following: "as a Cynic he spoke more harshly" (Cicero, *Tusc. Disp.* 1.43.104); "quick-tempered, uneducated, harsh-voiced, and abusive" (Lucian, *The Runaways* 27); referring to "Cynic blasphemy" (Plutarch, *De tranquillitate animi* 468a) and their capacity to "revile tactlessly" (Epictetus, 3.22.50). At times, undoubtedly, there was no way to write down what they said verbatim and remain within the bounds of "literary" language. But we are not completely lacking in examples of their "barking":

> Diogenes the Dog to the so-called Greeks: a plague on you! . . . For although to all appearances you are men, you are apes at heart. You pretend to everything, but know nothing. . . . It is not only the Dog that hates you; nature itself does, too. . . . Of course, they seemed to be guilty! But, you blockheads, should one not attempt to educate such people rather than kill them? For without doubt we have no need of corpses, unless we intend to eat them as the flesh of sacrificial victims. But there is most certainly a need for good men, you blockheads. . . . And, you blockheads, whomever you lay your hands on, you wrong and chastise. And yet you yourselves deserve greater punishment. . . . If you have any sense, as you do not when you are drunk, obey Socrates the wise and me, and come together in common council, all of you from the youth upward, and either learn self-control or hang yourselves. . . . If you indulge yourselves, and think about how many good things there are of which you are said to be the masters, the public executioners, whom you call doctors, will come to you. . . . I call a plague on you real barbarians, until you learn in the Greek way and become true Greeks. For now those who are called barbarians are much more refined both in the place where they live and in their way of life. . . . But nothing is enough for you, for you are lovers of glory, irrational, and ineptly brought up (Pseudo-Diogenes 28).

> Since you have resolved to take care of yourself, I will send a man to you who is not, by Zeus, like Aristippus and Plato, but is one of the paedagogues of Athens that I engage. He has very keen powers of vision, moves very swiftly, and carries a very painful whip. He will direct you, by Zeus, not to take your rest early, but to rise early, and will give you rest from your fears and terrors. . . . your companions do not see the extent of your evil, nor do you yourself perceive it, for so long and so thoroughly has the sickness gripped you. Consequently, you need a whip and an overlord and not someone who will admire and flatter you. Indeed, how would anyone ever be benefited from this sort of person, and how would such a person benefit anyone? Only if he were to chastise him like a horse or an ox and at the same time recall him to his senses and pay heed to what is lacking. But you are in an advanced stage of corruption. Therefore, cutting, cautery and medication must be employed (Pseudo-Diogenes 29).

> They wonder why Heraclitus is always sullen; they do not wonder why men are always evil. If you reduced your vice a little, I would quickly smile. And

> yet in my disease, I have now become gentler, because I do not meet men, but am ill all alone (Pseudo-Heraclitus 5.3).

Cynic *parrēsia* is best displayed, however, in those instances where brazenness and a belly-laugh combine to show how utterly unconstrained the Cynics were by contemporary standards of personal comportment. (The encounter between Alexander the Great and Diogenes was not without its humor.) In these instances, we also note how difficult it is finally to separate Cynic speech from Cynic action. Discursive formation and ascetic practice are here coterminus, being equally illustrative of Cynic *parrēsia*:

> But just as Diogenes, when someone was shoving him and twisting his neck while he was indisposed, did not submit but instead showed the fellow his penis, and says, "My dear sir, stand here in front of me and shove on this" (Teles 11H).
>
> Someone took [Diogenes] into a magnificent house and warned him not to spit, whereupon having cleared his throat he discharged the phlegm into the man's face, being unable, he said, to find a meaner receptacle (Diogenes Laertius 6.32).
>
> When someone first shook a beam at him and then shouted, "Look out," Diogenes struck the man with his staff and added, "Look out" (Diogenes Laertius 6.66).

These sayings make clear that before proceeding any further, we must now consider Cynic shamelessness.

2. Ascetic Practice as Anaideia

Like all ascetics, the Cynics trained (Foucault, 1985:73–74; Vaage:119–27). Like Hercules, their daily toil was the means whereby they labored toward felicity: *eudaimonia* (Hoïstad:22–73). But can we speak about a Cynic regimen? Not as a rule, in the strict sense of a set of prescriptions and proscriptions, but certainly as a tendency, a general *élan* or *afán*. Though this may seem to beg the question. Does everything the Cynics said and did belong to one basic strategy? Does not the diversity of Cynic words and deeds exemplify the fact that there were different "types" of them in antiquity (Malherbe:37–45)? And what if they were simply acting up? In this case, we would face in Cynicism just plain pandemonium: sheer antic chaos.

I want to argue that the Cynics were shameless ascetics. By this, I mean that their particular style of public display embodied a program of training in shamelessness (*anaideia*). Cynic *parrēsia* formed part of this larger endeavor, at the same time that it made whatever was done "signify" something. Without the discursive performance of "boldness of speech," Cynic acts of uncivilized behavior would simply have remained "out of place." On the other hand, without "outrageous" behavior to give it substance, Cynic speech would have remained so many loud but empty words.

A close relationship between Cynic *parrēsia* and the practice of *anaideia* was already apparent at the end of the preceding section. It is equally evident in the following Cynic epistles:

> One does not need to be grateful to one's parents, either for the fact that one was born, because what exists has been brought into being by nature, or for one's particular character, for the blending of the primal elements is the cause of this. And indeed, no thanks is needed even for the things done on purpose or intentionally. For birth is a consequence of making love, which is pursued for the sake of pleasure, not birth. These pronouncements I, the prophet of insensitivity, utter in opposition to the ignorant life. And if to some they appear too harsh, nature establishes them as true, as does the life of those who live not ignorantly but in accordance with virtue (Pseudo-Diogenes 21).

> My hand sounded the wedding hymn first before your arrival and it understood that the satisfaction of sexual pleasures was more easily procured than that of the stomach. For Cynicism, as you know, is an investigation of nature (Pseudo-Diogenes 42; cf. Diogenes Laertius 6.46, 69).

> Not only bread and water, a bed of straw, and a coarse cloak teach poise and hardiness, but, if one needs to speak this way, also a shepherd's hand. Would that I knew as well that man of yore who was a cowherd! Take care, therefore, also of this, wherever you hurry off to. For it has to do with the ordering of our life. And let uncontrolled intercourse with women go its way, which requires a lot of free time. For there is no free time, not only for a poor man to beg, according to Plato, but also for the person who is hurrying along the shortcut to happiness. Intercourse with women brings enjoyment to men—the uneducated many—who likewise, on account of this practice, must pay the price. You will learn with those who have learned from Pan to do it manually. Do not turn aside, not even if certain people on account of such a life call you a dog or something worse (Pseudo-Diogenes 44).

Here is "boldness of speech" inextricably combined with a determined shamelessness, just as at the other end of the spectrum could be found those whose "shameful" lives resulted from their lack of courage or ability to "speak boldly":

> For it is not, I think, because [Bellerophon] desired a higher place, but rather because he tried to do things that were beyond his power, that misfortunes later befell him. For having lost his hope, he lived the rest of his life shamefully and disgracefully, since he had gone out into the wilderness because of those who were insulting him in the towns, and had lost his foundation, which is not speaking as we are accustomed to, but is the boldness of speech upon which each person's life is set upright (Pseudo-Socrates 1.12).

Lest one think that the object of Cynic shamelessness was especially sexual reserve, as though its basic meaning were one of preaching "free love" to ancient Puritans, it is important to recognize that the types of declarations and demonstrative behavior cited above were accompanied in Cynicism by a correlative polemic against the use of courtesans and other standard forms of sexual behavior in antiquity (cf. Foucault, 1985; Julian 6.202a). Cynic shamelessness did not simply mean: If it feels good, do it (Foucault, 1985:54–55; cf. Pseudo-Diogenes 44). Thus we read:

> A youth was playing cottabos in the baths. Diogenes said to him, "the better you play, the worse it is for you" (Diogenes Laertius 6.46).
>
> To a young man who complained of the number of people who annoyed him by their attentions, [Diogenes] said, "Cease to hang out a sign of invitation" (Diogenes Laertius 6.47).
>
> Noticing a good-looking youth lying in an exposed position, [Diogenes] nudged him and cried, "Up, man, up, lest some foe thrust a dart into thy back!" (Diogenes Laertius 6.53).
>
> Libertines he compared to fig-trees growing upon a cliff: whose fruit is not enjoyed by anyone, but is eaten by ravens and vultures (Diogenes Laertius 6.60).
>
> Seeing an Olympian victor casting repeated glances at a courtesan, "See," [Diogenes] said, "yonder ram frenzied for battle, how he is held fast by the neck fascinated by a common minx" (Diogenes Laertius,6.61).
>
> Handsome courtesans he would compare to a deadly honeyed potion (Diogenes Laertius 6.61).
>
> Seeing the child of a courtesan throw stones at a crowd, [Diogenes] cried out, "Take care you don't hit your father" (Diogenes Laertius 6.62).
>
> The mistresses of kings [Diogenes] called queens; for, he said, they make kings do their bidding (Diogenes Laertius 6.63).
>
> Seeing a young man behaving effeminately, "Are you not ashamed," [Diogenes] said, "that your own intention about yourself should be worse than nature's; for nature made you a man, but you are forcing yourself to play a woman" (Diogenes Laertius 6.65).
>
> To a man who was urgently pressing his suit to a courtesan, [Diogenes] said, "Why, hapless man, are you at such pains to gain your suit, when it would be better for you to lose it?" (Diogenes Laertius 6.66).
>
> Being asked what was evil in life, [Diogenes] said, "A good-looking woman" (*Gnomologium Vaticanum* 189).
>
> [Crates] carried on a regular campaign of invective against the courtesans, habituating himself to meet their abuse (Diogenes Laertius 6.90).

Further examples of Cynic shamelessness unrelated generally to sexual activity include the following:

> At a feast certain people kept throwing all the bones to him as they would have done to a dog. Thereupon he played a dog's trick and drenched them (Diogenes Laertius 6.46).
>
> Being reproached for eating in the marketplace, "Well, it was in the marketplace," [Diogenes] said, "that I felt hungry" (Diogenes Laertius 6.53; cf. further, 6.61).

> [Diogenes] was gathering figs, and was told by the keeper that not long before a man had hanged himself on that very fig-tree. "Then," said he, "I will now cleanse it" (Diogenes Laertius 6.61).
>
> When someone reproached [Diogenes] for going into dirty places, his reply was that the sun too visits cesspools without being defiled (Diogenes Laertius 6.63).
>
> Being reproached with drinking in a tavern, "Well," said [Diogenes], "I also get my hair cut in a barber's shop" (Diogenes Laertius 6.66).
>
> It was [Diogenes'] habit to do everything in public, the works of Demeter and of Aphrodite alike (Diogenes Laertius 6.69).

The moral "success" of this kind of behavior depended upon the practitioner's ability to speak its unseemly truth in such a way that the conventional rejection of it would be held in check. In the same way, customary moral reasoning was also put in question. Basic to the inversionary strategy at work here is an extremely sharp sense of humor. Considerable skill at self-defense in the face of offended or anxious rebukers is also apparent. But the light-hearted laughter with which the Cynics managed to upset the moral apple-cart of their contemporaries, believing that the fruit it bore had gone bad, is most significant. Such lack of seriousness about the issues involved made the indicated acts of shamelessness even more entertaining, disarming, brazen, and sufficiently persuasive to be repeated time and again as examples of adroit repartee.

The Cynics' attitude toward burial demonstrates especially well the fusion of *parrēsia* and *anaideia* that marked their style of asceticism. A few examples must suffice:

> Diogenes was rougher; ... like a Cynic he spoke more harshly and required that he should be flung out unburied. Upon which his friends said: "To the birds and wild beasts?" "Certainly not," said he, "but you must put a stick near me to drive them away with." "How can you, for you will be without consciousness?" they replied. "What harm, then, can the mangling of wild beasts do me if I am without consciousness?" (Cicero, *Tusc. Disp.* 1.43.104).
>
> Being asked whether he had a maid or boy to wait on him, [Diogenes] said, "No." "If you should die, then, who will carry you out to burial?" "Whoever wants the house," he replied (Diogenes Laertius 6.52; cf. 6.79).
>
> Xeniades once asked [Diogenes] how he wished to be buried. To which he replied, "On my face." "Why?" inquired the other. "Because," said he, "after a little while, down will be converted into up." This because the Macedonians had now gotten the supremacy, that is, had risen high from a humble position (Diogenes Laertius 6.31–32).

Notably in the final saying, Alexander the Great is once again on the horizon. In the first example, Cicero moves directly from the statement, "like a Cynic he spoke more harshly," into a discussion of Diogenes' instructions for non-burial. Quick wit, strong syllogistic reasoning, and keen political analysis are evident in what was equally a posture of bald uncouthness. A developed style of discursive style defended and entertained the most primitive sort of social practice. Is the combination merely a sign of confused internal contradiction? Or was a more "meaningful" contrariness signaled thereby?

Despite the Cynics' considerable skill at retort, not everyone was convinced of their virtue. Cicero, for example, predictably refused to go along:

> But we should give no heed to the Cynics (or to some Stoics who are practically Cynics) who censure and ridicule us for holding that the mere mention of some actions that are not immoral is shameful, while other things that are immoral we call by their real names. Robbery, fraud, and adultery, for example, are immoral in deed, but it is not indecent to name them. To beget children in wedlock is in deed morally right; to speak of it is indecent. And they assail modesty with a great many other arguments to the same purport (Cicero, *De offic.* 1.35.128; see also 1.41.148).

In this case, nothing was actually done beyond the verbal mention of certain things. Nonetheless, in Cicero's opinion, utter shamelessness is apparently equivalent to "an assault on modesty." For Cicero, *parrēsia* = *anaideia*.

Julian the "apostate" Roman emperor defended Diogenes' uncultured ways as follows:

> On the other hand, when Diogenes made unseemly noises or obeyed the call of nature or did anything else of that sort in the marketplace, as they say he did, he did so because he was trying to trample on the conceit of the men I have just mentioned, and to teach them that their practices were far more sordid and insupportable than his own (Julian 6.202bc).

Without intending to do so, Julian admits that Diogenes' behavior was, indeed, "sordid and insupportable." But even so, his argument runs, this was far less the case than was true for the standard habits of many "upstanding" men and women in contemporary society.

In this regard, another saying about Diogenes is especially interesting:

> And he saw no impropriety either in stealing anything from a temple or in eating the flesh of any animal; nor even anything impious in touching human flesh, this, he said, being clear from the custom of some foreign nations (Diogenes Laertius 6.73).

What comes to the fore behind the highly shameless proposal of defiling sacred space and possible cannibalism is the Cynic posture of "cosmopolitanism" (cf. Diogenes Laertius 6.63, 72; Epictetus 1.9.1). It provides an intriguing antipode to the rejection of classical education with which we began our discussion of Cynic *parrēsia*. At the heart of Cynic shamelessness—motivating it?—would be appreciation of the fact of cultural relativity.

Cynic habits of speech and behavior inhabited a border region located at the interstices of the different cognitive and social systems known in the ancient Mediterranean world (cf. Rosaldo). In this murky realm, the Cynics "carried on," both as unreserved protagonists of a tactless cultural critique (*parrēsia*), and as the highly unorthodox paedagogues of a peculiar mode of "popular" philosophical inquiry (*anaideia*). What unites everything they said and did in a single strategy of discourse and ascetic practice, beyond their seemingly unbounded powers of contextual inventiveness, is the affirmative relationship to social marginality that virtually every instance of "bold speech" and Cynic "shamelessness" betrays. In word and deed, the Cynics transgressed all the traditional codes for a "good" life embodied by proper speech and fitting manners, claiming to find greater contentment not through a complete or "finished" ethical formation, but in a "natural" state subverting every norm. Cynic *parrēsia* and *anaideia* were thus two sides of a single scarred coin: a mode of personal training I propose we call the "asceticism of trangsgression."

3. An Asceticism of Transgression

A passage in Diogenes Laertius' account of Cynicism (6.69-71) strangely mirrors this essay's shape thus far. At the beginning of the indicated passage (6.69), we find the statement which I quoted at the start of section one: "Being asked what was the most beautiful thing in the world, [Diogenes] replied: *parrēsia*," followed by an anecdote. We then read, as cited above: "It was his [Diogenes'] habit to do everything in public, the works of Demeter and of Aphrodite alike," followed by additional examples of Cynic *anaideia*, concluding with the claim: "Many other sayings [of this sort] are attributed to him, which it would take too long to enumerate" (cf. John 21:25).

Some general observations are then made about *askēsis*, specifically, the benefits of bodily training, followed by these remarks:

> Nothing in life, however, [Diogenes] maintained, has any chance of succeeding without strenuous practice; and this is capable of overcoming anything. Accordingly, instead of useless toils men should choose such as nature recommends, whereby they might have lived happily. Yet such is their madness that they choose to be miserable. For even the despising of pleasure is itself most pleasurable, when we are habituated to it; and just as those accustomed to a life of pleasure feel disgust when they pass over to the opposite experience, so those whose training has been of the opposite kind derive more plea-

sure from despising pleasure than from the pleasures themselves. This was the gist of his conversation; and it was plain that he acted accordingly, adulterating currency in very truth, allowing convention no such authority as he allowed to natural right, and asserting that the manner of life he lived was the same as that of Heracles when he preferred liberty to everything (Diogenes Laertius 6.71).

I will comment shortly on this text. First, however, we might contrast with what has already been written about Cynic *parrēsia* and shamelessness the following observations by Peter Brown regarding the holy man in late (Syrian) antiquity:

Men entrusted themselves to him because he was thought to have won his way to intimacy with God—παρρησία. This word has a long history. It was only in Syria in the fourth century that it took on the final harsh contours that the word implied in Byzantine piety. For the παρρησία enjoyed by the Byzantine saint is subtly different from the delicate artifice of intimacy affected by rulers and their circle in Hellenistic times. It was a dizzy privilege, earned by a lifetime of tremulous obedience and hard work at the court of an absolute monarch [namely, God]. . . . The power so gained was the reward of service. The labours of the holy man echo the 'sweat'—the *sudor*—of the new nobility of service of the East Roman state (Brown:136).

Intriguing here is how what Brown writes about comes so close to, yet remains so far from, what was basically at stake in Cynic *parrēsia*. The key words are intimacy, obedience, and service. Cynic *parrēsia* was not the reward of obedience to a divine ruler, but one of the means whereby the conventional forms of virtuous comportment in ancient Hellenistic society were disobeyed for the sake of achieving, not intimacy, but a state of greater felicity equated with following nature. Cynic "boldness of speech" and its correlative behavior could be portrayed occasionally as performed in the service of other human beings (Bernays:101–102; Malherbe:42–45). But such service was never thought to be like that of a civil servant; it certainly did not echo life within the imperial Roman government. Rather, like the heroic works of Heracles, Cynic *parrēsia* and *anaideia* were conceived of as the acts of a liberating sovereignty. The Cynics were never, as Brown depicts the Syrian saints, by virtue of their ascetic labors the new power brokers of a changing civilization. Instead, from start to finish, the Cynics were stray dogs on the margins of their world, barking and doing whatever at the edge of town.

Geoffrey Galt Harpham has argued for an understanding of asceticism in which the "marginal concept" of temptation would have priority. At one point, this is done in explicit contrast to the notion of transgression:

As Foucault describes it, the concept of transgression bears a strong resemblance to temptation: "The limit and transgression depend on each other for whatever density of being they possess: a limit could not exist if it were absolutely uncrossable and, reciprocally, transgression would be pointless if it merely crossed a limit composed of illusions and shadows. But can the limit have a life of its own outside of the act that gloriously passes through it and negates it?" ("Preface to Transgression" 34). No, it cannot, and herein lies the difference between transgression and temptation. In the former, polarities are collapsed into each other; they provide no resistance, insist on no independence from each other. The difference between the two ideas is reducible to this: transgression is temptation minus resistance; as such, it is temptation's temptation (Harpham:59–60).

In the case of the Cynics, however, I would argue that their habits of transgression represent resistance minus temptation. Harpham contends that "In Foucault's terms, [temptation] makes possible the struggle against transgression by restoring, however minimally, the effectuality of thought, and therefore the possibility of resistance." I would contend that, in the case of the Cynics, the possibility of resistance is registered precisely by the struggle *for* transgression which restores, however minimally, the effectuality of thought in the form of *parrēsia*. But resistance to what? That is undoubtedly the critical question.

In Foucault's terms, as well as those of Harpham, it is the imposition/transgression of "the limit" that is resisted. Foucault opposes the right of the limit to restrict, Harpham the right of Foucault to render nugatory the meaningfulness of limitation. The debate is eminently ours, in the context of a cultural situation saturated, on the one hand, by legal and bureaucratic definition and, on the other, by ideals of individual freedom and self-realization. We live in a world for which a sense of the reality of "limits" is both a philosophical given since Kant and a moral imperative in the face of impending ecological disaster. Both Foucault and Harpham thus rightly assume the discursive facticity of "the limit" in their respective writings.

In the case of the Cynics, however, the reality of "the limit" was precisely not assumed. Whatever we may think about the real possibility of a "limitless" style, it is clear that we will not succeed in understanding Cynic asceticism if we merely assume that they too, of course, recognized "the limit" in some way. What they recognized instead was the diffusion of "opinion" (*doxa*): conventional social judgment enshrined in local customs and taboos (cf. Foucault, 1986:135–36). It was precisely because the Cynics did not accord any measure of reality to these scales of valorization and fear, seeing in them merely measures of confusion and dissatisfaction, that Cynic speech and behavior inevitably became the works of an asceticism of transgression, continually exceeding, digressing, and subverting existing "normal" patterns of life.

Cynic "transgression" was less a "criminal" crossing over of an imagined or inscribed line of containment, and more like the chthonic movement of children "criss-crossing" every attempted ordering of things, like excited puppies, never housebroken, wreaking havoc in the livingroom. The asceticism of transgression practiced by the Cynics was, therefore, returning to Diogenes Laertius (6.71): "adulterating currency in very truth, allowing convention no such authority as he [Diogenes] allowed to natural right, and asserting that the manner of life he lived was the same as that of Heracles when he preferred liberty to everything." Here was the height of happiness, according to the Cynics: the sheer pleasure equated with "natural right" of going against the current. Thus, Diogenes "used to go into the theatre when the rest were coming out. When asked why, 'This,' he said, 'is what I have been doing all my life'" (Diogenes Laertius 6.64).

Conclusion

The Cynics trained to transgress. Theirs was an asceticism of transgression. This included, *inter alia*, not observing ancient codes of proper speech and appropriate behavior. The Cynic virtues of *parrēsia* and *anaideia* embody one and the same logic of moral subversion, short-circuiting the tracks of conventional "civilized" reason and restraint to investigate what they felt were the underexplored regions of "nature," outrage and hilarity. At times, they appear to have been all over the map, precisely because they refused to accept a single location on it. Unable and perhaps unwilling just to leave it all behind, the Cynic style of speaking and the things they did nonetheless ensured that their position in ancient society could only be a marginal one. Nevertheless, their position was manifested par excellence in the middle of the marketplace where, in full view of all, a most brazen sort of contentment was displayed.

WORKS CONSULTED

Bernays, Jacob
    1879   *Lucian und die Kyniker*. Berlin: Wilhelm Hertz.

Brown, Peter
    1982   "The Rise and Function of the Holy Man in Late Antiquity." Pp. 103–52 in *Society and the Holy in Late Antiquity*. Berkeley: University of California Press.

Foucault, Michel
- 1985 *The Use of Pleasure*. Vol. 2 of *The History of Sexuality*. Trans. Robert Hurley. New York: Random House (Vintage Books edition, 1986).
- 1986 *The Care of the Self*. Vol. 3 of *The History of Sexuality*. Trans. Robert Hurley. New York: Random House (Vintage Books edition, 1988).

Harpham, Geoffrey Galt
- 1987 *The Ascetic Imperative in Culture and Criticism*. Chicago: University of Chicago Press.

Hock, Ronald F. and Edward N. O'Neil
- 1986 *The Chreia in Ancient Rhetoric. Vol. 1. The Progymnasmata*. Atlanta, GA: Scholars.

Hoïstad, Ragnar
- 1948 *Cynic Hero and Cynic King: Studies in the Cynic Conception of Man*. Lund: Carl Bloms.

Kinstrand, J. F.
- 1976 *Bion of Borysthenes: A Collection of the Fragments with Introduction and Commentary*. Stockholm: Almqvist & Wiksell.

Malherbe, Abraham J.
- 1989 *Paul and the Popular Philosophers*. Minneapolis: Fortress.

Rosaldo, Renato
- 1989 *Culture and Truth: The Remaking of Social Analysis*. Boston: Beacon.

Vaage, Leif E.
- 1990 "Cynic Epistles (Selections)." Pp. 117–28 in *Ascetic Behavior in Greco-Roman Antiquity: A Sourcebook*. Ed. Vincent L. Wimbush. Minneapolis: Fortress.

IN PRAISE OF NOBLE WOMEN:
GENDER AND HONOR IN ASCETIC TEXTS

Karen J. Torjesen
Claremont Graduate School

ABSTRACT

The discourse of praise of ascetic women is influenced by the institutionalization of honor in Greek and Roman societies and by the gender system of the ancient Mediterranean. Family and property form the bedrock of honor; public benefactions and publicly demonstrated virtues enhance both individual and family honor. Public inscriptions praise individuals for the honor of their families, their benefactions and their virtues. The discourse of praise of Christian ascetics touches on all these coordinates.

However, the gender ideology of the ancient Mediterranean locates woman in the private sphere and praises her for private virtues, especially chastity. Therefore when aristocratic women are praised in public inscriptions for their benefactions, they are also praised for private virtues. Christian writers praising ascetic women follow the same pattern, extolling their chastity.

The profile of the hero is premised on the male personality and male virtues. The same gender ideology describes the female personality as passive and weak and female virtue as chastity. Nevertheless, Roman society produced stories of women's heroic chastity, stories of women who suffered for the sake of their chastity. Christian communities also produced stories of women who suffered for their chastity. The heroism of these women provided a vocabulary for the praise of the chastity of ascetic women.

A society reveals its profoundest expectations and its highest ideals in the discourse of praise which it lavishes on the individuals it has selected to be models for the group. Yet there is more encoded in the language of praise than moral heights of human behavior. The configuration of a culture, its gender hierarchy, the ordering of its social classes and its political practices all shape the discourse of praise. In this essay the relatively new methodology of gender analysis will be appropriated for the study of ascetic texts praising women. Gender analysis attempts to differentiate between male and female experience. Behind this methodology lies the assumption that the organization of gender in any society—the assignment of different activities to men and women, the distinction between male and female nature, the discrimination between male and female virtue—will shape the social experience of men and women along different lines. The objective of gender analysis, then, is to illuminate the ways women's experience is shaped by the cultural construction of gender. In the process it becomes clear that male experience is also shaped by the cultural construction of gender in any society, hence the designation gender analysis.

This essay focuses on the discourse of praise of ascetic women. The first task prelimary to the interpretation of a historical discourse is to establish the cultural matrix in which the discourse is formed. The assumption of this essay is that the Roman institutionalization of honor forms the cultural matrix which gives rise to discourses of praise. The modes of honor, its rituals, the subjects who are honored, the persons bestowing honor, the witnessing audience, and the ethical content of honor are all presupposed in a discourse of praise and are shaped by the institutionalization of honor.

The second task preliminary to the interpretation of ascetic texts praising women is a gender analysis of honor. When Greek and Roman writers refer to a sexual division of labor they speak in terms of a polarity between *oikos* and *polis*, between household and city, between domestic life and public affairs. Household management (for the aristocracy this involved the running of estates) included supervision of slaves, the administration of the economic productivity and the rearing of family. This was woman's assigned role and the household and its environs constituted woman's space. By way of contrast, the city as a political society and the public spaces which surrounded its political institutions constituted a male domain. Political activity such as public speaking, debating, voting and holding public offices was male activity. This gender ideology of public and private domains influences the discourse of praise. For in the public–private gender ideology, public honor is a male affair and women are customarily praised for private virtues. When the Roman institutionalization of honor intersected with the public–private gender ideology, praise for female virtue became problematic. How can public male honors be reconciled with private female virtues? Although there were tensions between the public character of honor and the private role assigned to women, politically active women were publicly honored, and there were strategies for ameliorating the tension between public honor and private virtue. Christian writers praising ascetic women adopted these strategies and evolved some of their own.

Honor as a Social Institution

A first century inscription from Lycia praises one of its civic leaders:

The people of Arneae and vicinity, to Lalla daughter of Timarchus son of Diotimus, their fellow citizen, wife of Diotimus, son of Vassus; priestess of the Emperor's cult and gymnasiarch[1] out of her own resources, honoured

> five times, chaste, cultivated, devoted to her husband and a model of all virtue, surpassing in every respect. She has glorified her ancestors' virtues with the example of her own character. [Erected] in recognition of her virtue and good will (Lefkowitz and Fant, 157)

This inscription to Lalla was financed and commissioned by the city to acknowledge (and encourage) a benefactress who in taking the office of gymnasiarch also provided the budget for this center of civic life.

An inscription from Megalopolis from the second century BCE praises Euxenia for her benefactions to the city; she built a wall around the city's temple and an adjacent hostel for pilgrims to the temple. The city's praise begins with a description of her illustrious genealogy, lists her benefactions and concludes with the lines: "That a woman trades her wealth for a good reputation is not surprising, since ancestral virtue remains in one's children" (van Bremen, 223). Menodora was honored four times with inscriptions by the people of Sillyon. She had served the city by holding a number of public offices—magistracies, priesthoods and liturgies (offices which required donations to support public services.) A large donation to finance the distribution of grain to children, the construction of a temple, and gifts of cult statues were among her benefactions. The city had erected several statues of her which stood in the public places of the city (van Bremen, 223). In Bythinia Plancia Magna was honored because she built, at her expense, the large gate complex with its adjoining buildings that provided the magnificent entrance to the southern portion of the city (van Bremen, 235).

Honor is created by a complicated weaving of many factors. The strong lines of familial bonds formed the warp upon which the particular pattern of honor would be woven. Lalla is the daughter of Timarchus and the wife of Diotimus; she shared in the social worth ascribed to both of these families. The honor of a family reached back into a distant past encompassing the achievements of earlier generations. The collective honor of the past generations created a kind of social capital upon which a present generation could build. The city of Arneae praises Lalla because she "has glorified her ancestors' virtues with the example of her own character" (Pleket:13, Lefkowitz and Fant:157).

Only propertied families could lay claim to honor. The wealth gained in trading was suspect, but landholding established social worth. A member of a family who could lay claim to lineage and property was in a position to enhance her honor through patronage and benefactions. Assuming and financing a public office such as the gymnasiarchy was a form of patronage of a city. Building temples, repairing aqueducts, and providing grain for distribution were other forms of patronage. Through the use of wealth for civic service a member of the propertied classes could win a public acknowledgement of her virtue.

The profiles of honor that such a patron might hope to achieve were sketched with such terms as "excellence," "nobility," "generosity," "lover of honor," "just," "faithful" and "civic-minded" (Danker: 317–366). Lalla is "a model of all virtues, surpassing in every respect." The inscription and the monument that probably accompanied it was erected "in recognition of her virtue and good will." She had already received public honors five times.

A city council of Syros voted the following honors to Berenice:

> The resolution of the *prytaneis*, approved by the council and the people: whereas Berenice, daughter of Nichomachus, wife of Aristocles, son of Isidorus, has conducted herself well and appropriately on all occasions and after she was made a magistrate unsparingly celebrated rites at her own expense for gods and men on behalf of her native city, and after she was made priestess of the heavenly gods and the holy goddesses Demeter and Kore and celebrated their rites in a holy and worthy manner, she has given up her life—meanwhile she has also raised her own children. Voted to commend the span of this woman's lifetime to crown her with the gold wreath, which in our fatherland is customarily used to crown good women. Let the man who proposed this resolution announce at her burial: "The people of Syros crown Berenice daughter of Nichomachus, with a gold crown in recognition of her virtue and her goodwill towards them" (Kraemer, 217).

The illustrious Livia, wife of Augustus, received many public honors for her political service to Rome. She received a statue erected in her honor and the diplomatic immunity that those holding the office of tribune enjoyed. On her death the Senate erected an arch in her honor. The Senate's further desire to bestow on her the title of "Mother of the Country" and to grant her divine honors was frustrated by the opposition of her son, the emperor Tiberius (Dio 49.38; 60.46; 5.2). Tacitus remarked in an aside that "in fact he was fretted by jealousy and regarded the elevation of a woman as a degradation of himself" (Annals, 1. 14). What Tiberius said to the Senate, however, was that it was not proper for a woman to receive conspicuous public honors. With this comment he was quietly invoking the public–private gender system to deflect the public honors directed toward his powerful mother.

Public Men, Private Women

The gender system of the ancient Mediterranean articulated a sexual division of labor based on the experience of the property-holding classes. The origins of the Mediterranean public–private gender system can be traced back to the evolution of the democratic city-state. The concept of the *polis* set over against the *oikos* emerged during the period of the development of democratic political institutions. The creation of democratic political institutions required the capacity to think abstractly about political power. In effect, political power was abstracted from the person of the monarch, separated into various functions—military, economic and administrative—and invested in political institutions, such as the assembly and the council. In this process, a new domain was created which had not existed before—the domain of the *polis* or political life.

The warrior nobility, the *hippeis*, an equestrian elite, had been the ruling class of predemocratic, archaic Greece. The idea of the power shared by this ruling aristocracy was expressed in the concept of *isocratia*, meaning that all shared the same rule, in contrast to all power residing in the person of the absolute monarch. The creation of the *polis* in classical Greece represented a limited democratization of this rule by including as citizens (and therefore as part of the ruling class), the hoplites, armed foot soldiers, who were small landowners (Vernant, 38–68).

Prior to this transition, political power had been exercised within kinship systems, and so, within the family. This meant that women in the royal or ruling families would be able to participate in political processes, and might even inherit political offices. With the creation of a domain separate from the family in which political power was exercised, women were effectively excluded from political power.[2]

The public–private gender ideology expressed the ideals of the propertied classes. For men of the landholding classes, participation in public life provided a sense of identity. Economic life, management of the estate, production of cloth were relegated to the household, the domain that provided identity for women. Isomachus, a character in Xenophon's treatise on household management, had newly come into possession of an estate. When he was asked how he came to be called an aristocrat, he drew himself up to his full masculine height and declared that he did not concern himself at all with the household, for his wife was quite competent in the management of this sphere (*Oeconomicus* 7.3).

Philo, the Jewish apologist appeals to the same gender ideology to argue for the moral authority of the Jewish community:

> Market places and council halls and law courts and gatherings and meetings where large numbers of people are assembled and open air life will full scope for discussion and action—all these are suitable for men both in war and peace. Women are best suited for the indoor life which never strays from the house.... Organized communities are of two sorts: the greater which we call cities, and the smaller which we call households.... The government of the greater is assigned to men under the name of politics, and that of the lesser known as household management to women" (*The Special Laws* 3.169–170).

Men of the propertied classes who enjoyed the rights of citizenship defined themselves in terms of their participation in public life, office holding, debating, arguing in court and voting. Women of the same classes were defined by their exclusion from public life and their segregation within the domestic sphere. Philo continues: "A woman, then, should not be a busy body meddling with matters outside her household concerns, but should seek a life of seclusion" (*The Special Laws* 3, 169).

The public–private gender system was strengthened by a system of gendered ethics. To males were assigned the virtues of courage, justice, fortitude and temperance. Through the centuries, between the rise of the democratic city-state and the spread of the Roman Empire, these became the virtues associated with public life. The public-political domain of the citizen formed the stage on which men competed for honor. If a man's claim to honor was acknowledged, then the city in the collective voice of public opinion would rise up to praise him for the virtues of courage, justice, fortitude and temperance (Dill: 253). The traditional catalogue of women's virtues—chastity, silence and obedience—underlined their subordinate roles in their domestic relationships and did not apply to public life. In an essay *On Chastity*, a Greek writer explains:

> "courage, justice and intelligence are qualities that men and women have in common. Courage and intelligence are more appropriately male qualities because of the strength of men's bodies and the power of their minds. Chastity is more appropriately female."

The writer offers no justification for the latter; the assertion that chastity is a female virtue expressed one of the self-evident truths of his society (Lefkowitz and Fant: 104).

Women's Private Virtues

Nevertheless women of the aristocracy with resources of wealth and family connections were active in public life, and society ameliorated the tension of the clash between women's actual public roles and the public–private gender ideology by firmly wedding the public woman to private virtues. Whenever a woman's public roles were affirmed her private virtues were also praised, so that although a woman held public roles she excelled as a model of private virtues. A Roman eulogist speaking at the funeral of his mother explains that the "praise for all good women is simple and similar." (Women's praise is generic, for virtues they all share, while men are praised for their individual exploits.)

> "Sufficient is the fact that they have all done the same good deeds ... by necessity we pay tribute to the values they hold in common ... my dearest

mother deserved greater praise than all others, since in modesty, propriety, chastity, obedience, wool-working, industry and honor she was the equal of all good women (but competition was still necessary as a criterion for excelling . . .)"(Lefkowitz and Fant:136).

Here is the traditional catalogue of female virtues: chastity is the cornerstone, modesty and propriety and honor are all coordinates of this queen of the virtues.

Both men and women of the propertied classes used the wealth at their disposal to hold public office and to make public benefactions. When this generosity and civic-mindedness was publicly acknowledged by a city, wealth was thereby translated into public honors for both men and women. However male rhetoricians could use the public–private gender ideology to discredit individual women in public roles. This was Tiberius' tactic when he persuaded the Senate not to grant Livia the title, "Mother of the country." Judith Hallet remarks on the paradox created by this gender ideology:

> Many well-born women are remembered as possessing forceful personalities and exerting a substantial impact on men's public affairs . . . despite their society's extolling of domesticity as women's only proper concern and despite their own legal liabilities and formal exclusion from political participation (6).

Roman women were active in public life, but praised for private virtues. Riet van Bremen makes a similar observation about women in the municipal elites of the Greek cities:

> In seeming contradiction to the public activities and independent behavior of these women, the most frequent epithets used for women are to be found in exactly the traditional family areas of modesty, loving dedication to husband and family, piety and decency" (234).

Again public women are praised for private virtues.

Lalla, like the men of her social class, pursued honor through public service and received its rewards in the form of public acknowledgement of her social worth. However, unlike the men of her class, she is also praised for being chaste, cultivated and devoted to her husband. These are women's private virtues. Another daughter of the same Timarchus of Arneae was honored by her father with an inscription recording her honors from the city—a golden wreath and a bronze statue of herself. In this inscription Timarchus calls her "a woman who was chaste and cultivated and who glorifies both her city and her family with praise won for her conduct with recognition of her virtue and the incomparable and enviable manner with which she exemplifies every quality of womanhood" (Lefkowitz and Fant: 158).

Many aspects of honor were ungendered. The cumulative honor of an illustrious family was ascribed to all the heirs of that family name whether they were sons or daughters. Because sons and daughters were equally bearers of this social capital, the inscriptions mention the parents and ancestors of the woman as sources of her honor. Family honor could also be acquired through marriages and in these inscriptions the husband and his family are named. The practice of patronage was also ungendered; both men and women of the propertied classes used their wealth to benefit clients (individuals, cities, or ethnic groups) who in turn responded with public attestations of honor. The cities referred to here honored their patrons with inscriptions placed in conspicuous public centers which detailed the gifts of their benefactors. The benefactor's virtues of generosity and civic-mindedness were heralded in these public places; if the patron was a woman the private virtues of domesticity were also lauded.

Women, Honor and Asceticism

The term "nobility," as even the English suggests, refers simultaneously to a quality of character and a social class. In its earliest usage *aretē* signified the distinctive character of the warrior nobility of the archaic period. The term itself derives form *aristos* meaning superior—the collective plural *aristoi* designated the nobility as a social class, as the English term aristocracy also suggests (Kautsky: 169–177). The nobility of the ascetic women of the aristocracy lay as much in the honor their families possessed as in the virtues they achieved through ascetic renunciation.

Jerome, swept up into the whirlwind of his own rhetoric, calls virginity the road to nobility and public honors and reputation. "A virgin has to make a noble house more noble still by her virginity" (Jerome, Letter 130.6). Jerome goes on to assure Demetrias that "had you become a man's bride but one province would have known of you: while as a Christian virgin you are known to the whole world" (Jerome, Letter 130.6). Following a pattern we have seen in the inscriptions honoring women benefactors, admirers of ascetic women begin their literary eulogies with an account of the nobility of their families.

In a study of aristocratic ascetic women, Elizabeth Clark uses Ramsay MacMullen's grid for assessing a family's claims to honor. The three coordinates are: how far back does the family line go (the most illustrious families could trace their ancestry back to a deity or a hero, and could count many consuls and prefects among their predecessors); how much wealth; and how close to Rome did the family's origins lie (MacMullen: 122, 106). The aristocratic ascetic women considered by Clark, Paula,

Demetrias, Salvina, Marcella and Olympias, were able to make formidable claims to honor (Clark, 1979: 60-79).

When Christian writers praise aristocratic ascetic women they follow the culturally established patterns for the praise of women. The biographer of Olympias uses a flesh/spirit polarity to convey to the reader the claims to honor of Olympias' family without seeming to attach much importance to "worldly" glory. She was the daughter of a *comites*, descendent of a governor, engaged to a prefect of the city, and courted by a relative of Emperor Theodosius. In the Spirit, however, she was the true child of God and a bride of Christ (Clark, 1979: 2-3). Jerome's encomium of Paula begins on a similar note, "noble in family, she was nobler still in holiness"; she was a descendant of the Scipios and the Gracchi, a family that went back to Agamemnon, and her husband belonged to a family that claimed the Julii, and went back to Aeneas (Jerome, Letter 108). The biographer of Melania the Younger begins his narrative quite forthrightly: "The blessed Melania, then, was foremost among the Romans of Senatorial rank" and her husband came from a consular family (Clark, 1984: 27, 28). Jerome also begins his letter to Demetrias by praising her family's ancestry, the Probii and the Olybrii (Jerome, Letter: 130.3). In inscriptions praising women benefactors, the honor of the family is established first, the honor of the woman's ancestry, and then the honor of her husband's family. Christian writers praising ascetic women follow the same pattern. According to the etiquette of honor, the honor of ancestry must be praised first.

Like women of the propertied classes who won honor through benefactions, ascetic women of the aristocracy won fame for their benevolence through the rhetorical monuments raised by their biographers. After a short summary of her life, Olympias' biographer enthuses:

> For no place, no country, no desert, no island, no distant setting, remained without a share in the benevolence of this famous woman; rather, she furnished the churches with liturgical offering and helped the monasteries, and convents, the beggars, the prisoners, and those in exile; quite simply she distributed her alms over the entire inhabited world (Clark, 1979: 137).

Like other women of the propertied classes Olympias is praised for her benefactions and patronage, however in her case the grateful *politeia* is not the city, but the church in the person of bishops, ascetics and the poor. The extravagance of her biographer's praise is proportionate to the excess of her benefactions when compared to those of a civic patron.

Jerome praises Paula's benevolence extravagantly; indeed her benevolence was extravagant. Jerome asks: "What poor man as he lay dying was not wrapt in blankets given by her? What bedridden person was not supported with money from her purse? So lavish was her charity that she robbed her children" (Jerome, Letter 108.5). The benevolence of the ascetics was measured against two criteria, one was generosity to the *politeia*, the other was the resolve to liquidate fortunes in order to embrace poverty. Paula excelled especially in the latter and left her daughter a legacy of debt.

The benevolence of Melania the Younger and her husband received similar praise:

> For what city or country did not have a share in their enormously good deeds? If we say Mesopotamia and the rest of Syria, all of Palestine, the regions of Egypt and the Pentaopolis, would we say enough? When they acquired several islands they gave them to holy men. Likewise they purchased monasteries of monks and virgins and gave them as gifts to those who lived there (Clark, 1984: 41).

Like the benefactors of cities they financed buildings, and used their silver to make altars and liturgical implements with which they endowed churches.

Family and benevolence were aspects of honor that were ungendered, qualities easily praised in aristocratic women ascetics. However, the gendered aspects of honor, like the honor for wielding authority in matters of the public good, were as problematic for Christians writers as for their contemporaries. "Public" ascetic women were best praised for private virtues. Elizabeth Clark brings this problematic of female praise into focus in her article "Authority and Humility: A Conflict of Values in Female Monasticism" (1986). "Is not," she asks, "the Fathers' extravagant praise for the humility of their female subjects, when coupled with their deafening silence regarding the women's authoritative leadership, paradoxical?" (Clark, 1986: 209–210).

Three wealthy aristocratic women founded monasteries in the East— Olympias, Melania the Elder and Paula. Olympias established the first monastery in Constantinople and supervised and regulated the community of approximately 250 women. Melania the Elder founded monasteries for men and women on the Mount of Olives; the women's monastery housed fifty women. In Bethlehem Paula also established monasteries for men and women and directed the women's community. Yet the male admirers of female monasticism provide no details about the organization of the monastery, their governance, the rules that regulated community, or their economic operations.

Using Max Weber's *Economy and Society*, Clark suggests that "one possible explanation for "the Fathers" silence on the women as monastic leaders was that the authority they exercised was based neither on the offices they held, nor on the functions they performed, but on their personal status" (Clark, 1986: 214). Weber designates this kind of authority as patriarchal traditional authority in contrast to a rational/legal or charismatic type of authority. Traditional authority does not distinguish between public and private roles, nor between the leader's property and the property of the group. The loyalty of followers under traditional authority derives from their relationships as relatives, friends or slaves. Succession normally follows the lines of kinship, and authority does not operate through rules. Clark concludes that because the authority of female monastic founders was not dependent on office or rules, but rather family, wealth and status, the male historians of female monasticism failed to "mention the offices the women held, how they carried out their duty as superiors of convents or from what rules they derived their authority" (Clark, 1986:220).

Weber's description of traditional authority corresponds to another mode of leadership in Roman society—patronage. In this type of leadership power was based on wealth, loyalty, and relationships of dependency; and succession ran through kinship groups. This type of authority was based on personal authority rather than rules and linked public and private spheres. Patronage involved the exercise of political functions and the use of political power through: the patronage of persons of lower social classes; the patronage of foreign communities; and the *amicitia* form of patronage among the senatorial and equestrian classes (Eisenstadt and Roniger:52–53). The networks of patronage during the period of the late Roman empire constituted a structural element of Roman bureaucratic government and were an important avenue for exercising political leadership.

However, here too, the silence surrounding women's patronage is deafening. Roman historians leave no details about women's political leadership, neither their political objectives, nor their strategies for achieving them. We only have their cameo appearances in the lives and politics of Roman men. Yet the activities of men wielding the power of patronage are detailed and their achievements are lauded in Roman society and in Christian communities. Even in the case of male founders of monastic communities, far more attention is paid to their political authority than to the political authority of female founders of monastic communities.

The silence of male proponents of female monasticism about the leadership activities of artistocratic ascetic women can also be accounted for by Roman gender ideology: Women are to be praised for private virtues, but not for public activities. When they are lauded for public achievements it is their benevolence that is highlighted, not their exercise of authority.[3]

The conversion to asceticism was praised as a conversion to the old-fashioned Roman value of female chastity. Female chastity lay not so much in the renunciation of sexuality—the feature that was so central to male chastity in the ascetic movement—but rather had to do with the *appearance* of chastity. In this context "appearance" does not signify superficiality, but refers to a serious concern for one's public reputation for chastity.

Grooming, makeup and the choice of clothes were ways by which a woman could make a public demonstration of chastity. Seneca praises his own mother's unflinching loyalty to the virtue of chastity.

> Unchastity, the greatest evil of our time has never classed you with the great majority of women: jewels have not moved you, nor pearls ... you have not defiled your face with paints and cosmetics: never have you fancied the kind of dress that exposed no greater nakedness by being removed. In you has been seen that peerless ornament, that fearless beauty on which time lays no hand, that chiefest glory which is modesty (Lefkowitz and Fant: 140).

A woman could publicly demonstrate her chastity by avoiding the ostentation of jewelry, the falsification of cosmetics and by dressing in sturdy fabric of unassuming white.

One of the ancient treatments of the theme of chastity enumerated the five elements of a woman's chastity: 1) "the witness of her children to her chastity toward her husband" (they should look like him); 2) her clothes should be of plain fabrics and white (no silks, no colors), "no artificial coloring on her face" (no make-up), and no gold or emeralds or other jewels; 3) her seclusion in her home, no nocturnal visits, nor evening calls, if an expedition is necessary, then in the company of a slave; 4) no attendance at religious festivals that encourage drinking; and 5) "her readiness and moderation in sacrificing to the gods" (Lefkowitz and Fant:104). Since these were the forms for the public demonstration of chastity, writers praising ascetic women make much of Christian renunciation of clothes, make-up and jewelry.

Jerome allows Paula's own words to stand as evidence for her chastity: "I must disfigure that face [through penitential weeping] which contrary to God's commandment I have painted with rouge, white lead and antimony. I must exchange my soft linen and costly silks for rough goat's hair." Jerome rests his case: "Were I among her great and signal virtues to select her chastity as the subject of praise my words would seem superfluous" (Jerome, Letter 108.15). Demetrias' conversion to chastity is also ritualized through divesting herself of her jewels and her silks (Jerome, Letter 130).

Syncletica's biographer connects her conversion to chastity with the same symbols:

the weave of multicolored clothing did not seduce her eye, nor the different colors of precious stones ... At that time she put away from herself all cosmetics for it was the practice for women to call the hair the "cosmos" (a symbol for worldliness). This was the symbol that she had become a simple and pure being. Then for the first time she was deemed worthy of the name "virgin" (Castelli, 1990:270–271).

The biographer of Olympias is just as eager to praise her chastity by appeal to the same cultural symbols: "She had a life without vanity, an appearance without pretence, character without affectation, a face without adornment." Olympias exemplifies the traditional female virtues of chastity and modesty because her clothes are plain and she wears no makeup. Her biographer exalted her chastity and muted the reality of female authority (Clark, 1979:138)

A woman's seclusion was also a public sign of her chastity. Of Syncletica it is said, that "from her youth until her prime not only did she flee the society of all men, but she also for the most part avoided women" (Castelli, 1990:272). The writer of the *Life of Olympias* praises the seclusion of the female monastics, who received neither male nor female visitors (except John Chrysostom). In fact, it was the lack of seclusion that opened the way for accusations to be made against John Chrysostom, as well as against Olympias herself (Clark, 1979:133–134). Jerome urges seclusion on Eustochium, Paula's virgin daughter—no round of visits to other women, no attendance at nocturnal services held at the shrines of saints. Eustochium should keep to the "privacy of her own chamber" (Jerome, Letters 22,25, 16, 17). These practices provided convincing public evidence of female chastity.

Like their pagan counterparts, male Christian writers are not only silent on women's public authority, they are also effusive about women's private virtues. These writers, praising ascetic chastity, used the cultural symbols of the repudiation of fine clothes, cosmetics, and jewelry and ascetic seclusion to call attention to the chastity and virtue of ascetic women. Whether Roman society recognized in the ascetic woman the matronly chastity that it claimed to admire, or a caricature of it, is another question.

Masculinity and Honor

Not only was honor public, it was also masculine. The aggressive quest for honor, the willingness to compete for it, and the determination to avenge dishonor, defined the masculine character. In the gender system of ancient Mediterranean society males were socialized to compete for honor. The quest for honor was agonistic. Every social interaction taking place in this society witnessed by a "public" was viewed as a contest for honor—a dinner invitation, a gift, an arranged marriage. The arbitrator of honor was public opinion. Like the Greek chorus, the "public" was the anonymous audience for acts of honor; it deliberated and weighed claims to honor and gave its collective judgment. Although both men and women aspired to honor as a social good, the aggressive quest for honor had a distinctly masculine cast.

For members of the propertied classes competing for honor, such events were treated as a claim to honor that must be either accepted or rejected. A rival could effectively damage a competitor's honor by slandering his or her reputation, since reputation itself constituted one's social personality of honor. Not surprisingly, those traits which identified a truly masculine character—a desire for precedence and a willingness to defend one's reputation—were the traits essential for success in the competition for honor.

By contrast, the feminine character was defined in terms of a preoccupation with chastity. Sexual exclusiveness, timidity, shyness, obedience, submission and passivity were the desired attributes of the feminine personality. The Mediterranean socialization of girls focused on those traits of personality necessary to preserve chastity—a sense of shame, a concern for reputation, and passivity rather than aggressiveness. While maleness was equated with the pursuit of honor, femaleness was associated with preservation of shame.

Femaleness and Honor

A woman's honor was closely tied to her sexuality. What established a woman's honor was her public reputation for the virtue of chastity. The strategies by which a woman secured her reputation for chastity were varied. Because public space was male space—marketplaces, temples and festivals—a woman was careful that her appearance in public male space did not suggest any openness to encounter with men. She wore a veil, she would never travel alone, but in the company of slaves, and she would not go out during times when there was a press of people on the streets or at night. A woman who had no concern for her public reputation was shameless. "Shame is an inevitable part of being female, a woman is honorable if she remains cognizant of this fact and its implications for behavior and she is shameless if she forgets it" (Delaney:40).

Where the gendered values of honor and shame intersected with the Roman institutions of honor a dilemma was posed by female virtue. If female virtue is focused on chastity and characterized by passivity, how can it be dressed in the warrior-like clothes of male honor? Nevertheless the demand for feminine models of the heroic (and their popularity) did produce stories of female heroes—stories of women who defended their chastity heroically. In these stories the dilemma of female virtue is especially poignant. How does the storyteller derive heroic action out of the passive virtue of chastity? Christian writers praising ascetic women face the same dilemna.

Maleness in Mediterranean culture symbolized the quest for precedence, aggressiveness in competition and a willingness to defend one's reputation. These are the active aspects of the pursuit of honor. On the other hand femaleness functioned as a symbol for the passive aspects of honor, the concern to preserve a reputation. The reputation for honor that a woman must preserve was a reputation for chastity. The women of the propertied classes who were able to pursue and compete for public honor understood at the same time their symbolic role of signifying shame.

Livia, the wife of Augustus, one of the most powerful political figures in first century BCE Rome affirmed her female role of symbolizing shame central to her political power. The historian Dio reported with admiration:

> "when someone asked how and by what course of action she had obtained such a commanding influence over Augustus, she answered that it was by being scrupulously chaste herself, by doing whatever pleased him and not meddling with any of his affairs [the private ones!] and in particular by pretending neither to hear nor to notice any of the favorites who were the objects of his passion." (Dio, 58.2).

In this way Livia used her chastity as her legitimation of her public political role. An incident in which a chance encounter with some naked men [probably athletes] provided her again a public forum for affirming her chastity. She saved them from being executed—they had in effect violated her chastity—by saying that to chaste women such men were no whit different than statutes.

The anthropological work on which these descriptions of the honor and shame model are based are contemporary ethnographic descriptions of Mediterranean cultures. Bruce Malina has pioneered the use of cultural anthropology for the interpretation of New Testament texts.[4] He makes extensive use of the honor/shame value system for interpreting the social world of the New Testament writings. Although many scholars have appropriated aspects of the honor/shame model to interpret ancient Mediterranean societies, a thorough treatment of the honor/shame paradigm in classical societies is still wanting. Nevertheless a story from Livy reveals the presence of an honor and shame code in classical Roman society.

The story of Lucretia was told and retold offering her as the paradigm for female virtue. Lucretia was much admired for defending her reputation for chastity and modesty with the price of her life. The story itself exposes the problematic around female virtue. At a drinking party outside of Rome hot-headed young men competed with each other for honor by each claiming that his wife was the most virtuous. They agreed to settle the dispute by surprising their wives at their evening activities. While the wives of the other competitors were discovered at lavish dinner parties, Lucretia, the wife of Collatinus, was discovered at home still working on her wool. Because her conduct avoided all appearances of sexual indiscretion, "the prize of womanly virtues fell to Lucretia" (Livy, I.57). Since male honor was linked to female chastity Lucretia's husband, Collatinus, was designated "the victorious husband."

However, one of the competitors, Sextus Tarquinius, having been defeated in this contest of honor, determined to avenge his lost honor by depriving Lucretia of her honor—her chastity—and depriving Collatinus of his honor—Lucretia's chastity and sexual fidelity. While Collatinus was away, Sextus Tarquinius paid a visit to the chaste Lucretia and was graciously received as a friend of Collatinus. When the household was fast asleep Tarquinius with sword in hand made his way to Lucretia's chamber. First Tarquinius tried seduction, but Lucretia was unmoved in her chastity; then he threatened to kill her if she would not sleep with him. She was still resolute in her chastity. Finally he threatened to destroy her reputation by saying that when she was dead he would kill his slave and leave the naked body by her side and claim that he had put her to death in the act of adultery with a slave. "At this dreadful prospect her resolute modesty was overcome as if with force by his victorious lust. And Tarquinius departed exulting in his conquest of a woman's honor" (Livy I.57–58).

Lucretia then revealed the crime to her father and husband (the two men whose honor was at stake in her dishonor) and secured from them a promise to punish the adulterer. The honor of Lucretia's father and husband had been damaged, but it could be restored by their avenging themselves on the man who had wounded their honor. Lucretia's honor could not be restored; it had not only been damaged, it had been destroyed. Lucretia answers the worried inquiry of her father and husband, "Is all well?" with the bitter reply, "What can be well with a woman when she has lost her honor" (Livy I. 58). Unlike male honor which was achieved through a series of contests with other men, female honor could not be won, but only lost. The boundaries of woman's sexual body marked the boundaries of her honor. If those boundaries were penetrated, her honor was irretrievably lost. In her last speech, which conveyed for Roman society the trembling power of female chastity, Lucretia declared: "Although I acquit myself of the sin, I do not absolve myself of the punishment; nor in time to come shall ever unchaste woman live through the example of Lucretia" (Livy, I.58.10). When she finished this speech she drew her knife from beneath her robe and plunged it into her breast. Livy's story has ended; the denouement has been reached. For Romans the supreme value of female chastity was underlined in blood.

The public account of Lucretia's rape could have easily become a story of her seduction. In life Lucretia would have been a model of the seduced woman; in death she becomes the model of the chaste woman. Lucretia had found a way to redeem her honor and restore her reputation for chastity, but it was at the price of her life. Lucretia's father and brother could defend their honor by raising their hands against another. Lucretia could only defend her honor by raising her hand against herself.

For Christian women as well, chastity constituted the highest form of female honor; and for Christian women as well, chastity meant preserving the boundaries of the female sexual body. If this boundary were ever penetrated, then female honor would be irretrievably lost. And like Lucretia, Christian women valued female honor more than bodily life. When Alaric's warriors breached the gates of Rome and swept through the city for an orgy of burning, looting and raping, Christian women took their own lives rather than have their honor violated. Augustine struggles with feeble arguments to reverse this deep cultural intuition that the meaning of female chastity is the preservation of the boundaries of the female sexual body.[5]

Heroic Chastity

The figure of Lucretia represents a contorted convergence of female and male ideals. In its normal context the female virtue of chastity is passive, defensive and cautious. It is a virtue achieved by the avoidance of action. Yet in Livy's popular story Lucretia's chastity acquires a heroic dimension. Her chastity is demonstrated and sealed in a single decisive act. The act itself manifests all those characteristics admired in the heroic ideal.[6] In her single act Lucretia demonstrated courage, resolution, fearlessness and a heroic mastery over the body. The message of her action which struck such a responsive chord in Roman society was that female chastity is an ultimate value, worth the price of a woman's life.

Another popular form of literature, the Hellenistic novel, explored and celebrated the female virtue of chastity. Beautiful young women from aristocratic families are suddenly separated by fate from their lovers. They undergo the severest of trials—kidnapping, slavery and torture—and through it all retain their chastity out of their loyalty and love for their husbands or fiancés.[7] These stories have happy endings because their heroines are united with their lovers and marriage can begin at last.

The sufferings of these beautiful women on behalf of their chastity reach the dimension of the heroic, but it is a heroism of passive endurance, rather than a heroism of decisive action. Even when uprooted from their own country, they carefully observe the proprieties of public and private spaces and do not undertake a search for their lovers or make attempts to rescue themselves. Yet this in itself is a demonstration of their chastity.[8] They are presented as heroes to be admired for their courage and their fortitude and it is for the sake of the virtue of chastity that they have suffered.

The early Christian community produced a genre of its own celebrating female chastity—what Virginia Burrus calls the "Chastity Stories" of the Apocryphal Acts. In these engaging narratives beautiful, aristocratic women become enamored of the apostolic preaching of chastity. In response to the teachings of these wandering ascetics, they renounce sexual relations with husbands, masters and fiancés. In the end they defend their right to chastity against these men who have legitimate claims on their sexuality by protesting that they are already married to Christ. They further argue that their sexuality belongs to Christ and can be legitimately denied to the men of flesh and blood who by society's norms had sexual rights in them.[9]

While the stories of both genres celebrate female chastity, the striking difference between the chastity stories and the Hellenistic romances is their attitudes toward the institution of marriage as the proper haven for female sexuality. The resistance of the women in the chastity stories to the social institution of marriage takes on heroic dimensions as enormous pressures are brought to bear upon them by families and magistrates. Their heroism lies in their resistance to the culturally legitimate claims of parents, husbands and governors. Although the Christian heroines appropriate the cultural symbols of chastity by divesting themselves of fine clothing, jewelry and cosmetics, they flagrantly violate the rules of seclusion by moving freely about public space, even at night. One of the ironies of their stories is that although they are accused of being unchaste when they appear in public, they are in fact suffering for their chastity.

For the Christian community the Thecla story presented the most dramatic portrait of heroic chastity.[10] Thecla, a new devotee of Christian chastity, refused the importunate pleas of her fiancé Thamyris; she stubbornly stood her ground in the face of angry threats from her mother. When her furious mother appealed to the governor, Thecla defied the governor. Finally Thecla's enraged mother urged him to execute her by burning her as a warning to other young women. Thecla was miraculously saved from the fire. On later travels when a high official attempted to rape her, she successfully repulsed his advances by tearing his cloak and publicly shaming him. He appealed to the governor and demanded that Thecla be punished; she was sentenced to the wild beasts in the arena. Once again Thecla was divinely rescued. Her story ends as she devotes the rest of her life to traveling, preaching and baptizing. Here is a more active, hence a more heroic portrayal of female chastity. But it was won at the price of one of the most important symbols of chastity, that is, preserving the boundaries between public and private space.

It was this ideal of heroic chastity that allowed Christian writers to present ascetic women as heroic in the face of the dilemma that female virtue in itself was not heroic, nor did the basic description of the female personality (timidity, shyness, passivity) lend much material for the construction of the heroic. Jerome is sensitive to the dilemma of praising women and writes, "An unbelieving reader might perhaps laugh at me for laboring so long over the praises of ladies . . . but we judge moral excellences not by people's sex, but by their quality of spirit" (Jerome, Letter 127.5).

The Life of Olympias opens with exploits of Christian heroes—Abraham, Lot, Joseph, Job—culminating with Thecla, a "noble combatant" who received the crown. Olympias "walked in her footsteps." The biographer of Syncletica calls her the true disciple of Thecla: "For no one was ignorant of the martyrdoms of the blessed Thecla . . . and I think that many people will not escape noticing the virtuous and sweaty suffering of this one [Syncletica]" (Castelli, 1991:269). In a surprising twist at the end of this eulogy, this biographer places Syncletica ahead of Thecla: for the enemy attacked the latter "from the outside" while Syncletica's victory was over a "more piercing evil . . . opposing and destructive thoughts" (Castelli, 1991:270). In the Thecla story there is a blending of two motifs—martyrdom and chastity. It is Thecla's martyrdom, her sufferings in the arena, first by fire and then by beasts, which manifest the heroic. And these heroic sufferings are for the sake of her chastity. The blending of these two themes creates the Christian motif of heroic chastity. It is the combination of her martyrdom and her chastity that makes her the ideal prototype for the ascetics Olympias and Syncletica.

Christians constructed the meaning of martyrdom through a process anthropologists call reversal. In the actual experience of martyrdom the martyr was a victim of Roman justice and a victim of fire or beasts (in the case of citizens, of the executioner's sword). Christian discourse transformed the meaning of martyrdom by interpreting it through the metaphor of the arena, specifically gladiatorial combat. In this setting the quest for honor included the ultimate stakes of life and death. There was a contest, competition, and combat, in which one man conquered another, received the victor's crown and gained both honor and life. In effect the arena recapitulated the code of warriors in battle; this was a completely masculine world. In the Christian reconstruction of martyrdom, the martyr was a combatant; his or her opponent was the devil. When this enemy was vanquished by fearless dying the martyr received the victor's crown on the other side and honor from the Christian community on this side. In this Christian reversal the victim became victor.

This construction of martyrdom, because it was metaphoric, was ungendered. Both men and women suffered martyrdom and the metaphor of martyrdom as combat could be applied to men and women. The masculinity of this metaphor, coming as it does from warfare and the arena, meant that women could be praised for masculine attributes. In this way women seemed to have transcended both female virtue and the feminine personality. Syncletica is described as "trained sufficiently in sufferings, and having been led to the very height of the stadium" (Castelli, 1991:271). Of the young women and men that Melania the Younger converted to a life of chastity, her biographer writes that they "zealous for purity ... leaped into the arena of virtue" (Clark, 1984:47). Melania herself is described as "conquering the pleasures of the body and delivering herself daily to death" (Clark, 1984:35). The glossary of praise for ascetic women included the terms fearless, bold, despising weakness, and apt for contest, combat, victory, conquest—all of which allowed biographers to praise women for virtues that were essentially masculine.

In the end, because the heroic virtues were masculine and only the masculine character was praiseworthy, Christian writers praised ascetic women for possessing a "masculine" character and for performing "manly" deeds (Castelii, 1986:72–88). Syncletica is praised for her seclusion because she did not want people to be heralds of her "manly" deeds (Castelli, 1991:272). Olympias is praised for her ragged clothing as "coverings unworthy of her manly courage" (Clark, 1979:139). And the biographer of Melania the Younger bemoans his lack of rhetorical skill to "recount the manly deeds of this blessed woman."

The gender ideology of the ancient Meditteranean placed severe constraints on the praise of women. Circumscribed within the private sphere of domestic life, held accountable for the private virtues of chastity, silence and obedience, and molded by the cultural construction of the feminine personality (comprising shyness, timidity and restraint), women were unlikely subjects for the public praise of public virtues. The public arena of praise was a male domain, the public virtues were masculine virtues, firmly rooted in the masculine character.

Responding to the restraints of the gender ideology of the ancient Mediterranean, Christian writers evolved several strategies for praising ascetic women: On many points the discourse of praise of aristocratic ascetic women followed the discourse of praise of their counterparts who were active in civic life. Both groups of women were praised for the honor of their families and for their benefactions. However, rather than call attention to their public authority, their admirers praised them for their private virtues. For this reason Christian writers praising ascetic women wax eloquent on the culturally recognized symbols of chastity, the renunciation of elaborate clothes, the refusal to wear make-up and disavowal of jewelry on the part of ascetic women.

By borrowing the motif of heroic chastity and suffering for the sake of chastity, the discourse of praise of ascetic women circumvented the contraints of the heroic being firmly rooted in the male character and masculine virtues. By identifying asceticism as a form of martyrdom they were able to highlight its heroic dimensions for women. Thecla of the "Chastity Stories" provides the model for the linkage between asceticism and martyrdom for women. Women ascetics were martyrs and the discourse of praise could draw on the whole vocabulary of heroism in the martyr literature.

But at bottom the heroic was still masculine and rooted in the masculine character. So it is not surprising that in the end Christian writers praised ascetic women for having transcended the feminine personality. In the absence of cultural paradigms for female agency and female acheivement, successful women could only be praised for being "masculine."

NOTES

[1] The office of gymnasiarchy involved the maintenance of the *gymnasion* which functioned as a civic center for citizen males.

[2] The same process took place also in the fourteenth century, when political power was transferred from the feudal nobility to the political sphere of the towns constituted by the new merchant and trade class. This transfer of political power from kinship units to a separate public sphere was also the basis for the exclusion of women from political power. Following the American Revolution the founders of the democratic republic created a separate political domain that excluded freeborn women and male and female slaves. Citizenship was restricted to freeborn, propertied males.

[3] It is interesting to note that when a female writer discusses female monasticism political authority is highlighted. "Sergia's Narration" does emphasize the administrative work of Olympias, her predecessor: "but also up to the present she has not ceased in a formidable manner, by appearing in wondrous visions, to oversee, consider, shelter, and govern her monastery in all things, and as has been said, the souls who were in it" (Clark, 1979:150).

[4] *The New Testament World: Insights from Cultural Anthropology* (Atlanta: John Knox, 1981).

[5] Augustine, *City of God* I.16-18. Augustine argues that chastity is a matter of the mind, not of the body. If the intention to remain chaste is overwhelmed by violence, the raped woman should still regard herself as chaste.

[6] Suicide through the use of a knife or weapon was a male form of death. The traditional mode of suicide for women was hanging. See Nichole Loraux, *Tragic Ways of Killing Women*, trans. Anthony Forster (Cambridge: Cambridge University Press, 1987).

[7] See Chariton's *Chaereas and Callirhoe*, Ephesus' *An Ephesian Tale* and Achilles Tatius' *Leucippe and Clitophon*.

[8] I am indebted for some of these insights to Matt McCabe's master's thesis, "Two Heroines: Callirhoe and Thecla," Claremont Graduate School, 1993.

[9] Burrus argues that the chastity stories do not belong to the genre of the Hellenistic novel, but rather are legends presented as real events about historical persons and need to be analyzed with the methodologies of folklore. *Chastity as Autonomy* (Lewiston: Edwin Mellen Press, 1989).

[10] See Acts of Paul and Thecla, *New Testament Apocrypha*, Ed. E. Hennecke and W. Schneemelcher, trans. R. Wilson (London: Luterworth Press, 1965).

WORKS CONSULTED

Brown, Peter
    1988   *The Body and Society*. New York: Columbia University Press.

Castelli, Elizabeth
    1986   "Virginity and Its Meaning for Women's Sexuality in Early Christianity." *JFSR* 2:61–88.
    1990   "Pseudo-Athanasius. *The Life and Activity of the Holy and Blessed Teacher Syncletica*." Pp. 265–311 in *Ascetic Behavior in Greco-Roman Antiquity*. Ed. Vincent L. Wimbush. Minneapolis: Fortress.

Clark, Elizabeth
    1979   "The Life of Olympias" and "Sergia's Narration." Pp. 106–157. in *Jerome, Chrysostom and Friends*. Lewiston: Edwin Mellen.
    1984   *The Life of Melania the Younger*. Studies in Women and Religion 14. New York: Edwin Mellen.
    1986   "Piety, Propaganda, and Politics in the *Life of Melania the Younger*" Pp. 61–94 in *Ascetic Piety and Women's Faith*. Lewiston: Edwin Mellen.
    1986   "Authority and Humility: A Conflict of Values in Fourth-Century Female Monasticism." Pp. 209–28 in *Ascetic Piety and Women's Faith*. Lewiston: Edwin Mellen.

Danker, Frederick W.
    1982   *Benefactor: Epigraphic Study of Graeco-Roman and New Testament Semantic Field*. St. Louis: Clayton.

Delaney, Carol,
    1987   "Seeds of Honor, Fields of Shame." Pp. 35–48 in *Honor and Shame and the Unity of the Mediterranean*. A Special Publication of the American Anthropological Association 22. Washington, DC: American Anthropological Association.

Dill, Samuel
    1956   *Roman Society from Nero to Marcus Aurelius*. Cleveland: World.

Eisenstadt, S.N. and L. Roniger
    1984   *Patrons, Clients and Friends*. Cambridge: Cambridge University Press.

Elshtain, Jean Bethke
    1981   *Public Man, Private Woman*, Princeton: Princeton University Press.

Giovannini, Maureen J.,
    1987   "Female Chastity Codes in the Circum-Mediterranean: Comparative Perspectives" Pp. 61–74 in *Honor and Shame and the Unity of the Mediterranean*. Ed. David D. Gilmore. Special Publication of the American Anthropological Association 22. Washington, DC: American Anthropological Association.

Hallett, Judith
    1984   *Fathers and Daughters in Roman Society*. Princeton: Princeton University Press.

Jerome
    1954   *The Principle Works of Jerome*. Trans. W. H. Fremantle, G. Lewis, W.G. Martley. ANPNF Vol VI, 2nd Ser. Grand Rapids: Eerdmans.

Kautsky, J.
    1982   *The Politics of Aristocratic Empires*. Chapel Hill: University of North Carolina Press.

Kramer, Ross
    1988   *Maenads, Martyrs, Matrons, Monastics*. Philadephia: Fortress.

Lefkowitz, Mary R. and Maureen B. Fant
    1982   *Women's Life in Greece and Rome*. Baltimore: Johns Hopkins University Press.

Livy
    1919   *The Early History of Rome.* Volume 1, Trans. B. O. Foster. LCL. London: Cambridge University Press.

Loraux, Nichole
    1987   *Tragic Ways of Killing Women.* Trans. Anthony Forster. Harvard: Harvard University Press.

MacMullen, Ramsay
    1974   *Roman Social Relations.* New Haven: Yale University Press.

Pleket, H. W.
    1969   *Epigraphica.* Vol. II. Texts for the Social History of the Greek World.
            Textus Minores. Vol. XII. Leiden: E.J. Brill.

Rosaldo, Michelle Zimbalist
    1974   "Woman, Culture and Society: A Theoretical Overview." Pp. 17–42 in *Woman, Culture and Society.* Ed. Michelle Zimbalist Rosaldo: Stanford: Stanford University Press.

Torjesen, Karen
    1993   *Sex, Sin and Woman.* San Francisco: Harper Collins.

van Bremen, Riet
    1977   "Women and Wealth." Pp. 223–233 in *Images of Women in Antiquity.* Ed. Averil Cameron and Amelie Kuhrt. Detroit: Wayne State University Press.

Vernant, Jean Pierre
    1962   *The Origins of Greek Thought.* Ithaca: Cornell University Press.

THE DEFENSE OF THE BODY AND THE DISCOURSE OF APPETITE: CONTINENCE AND CONTROL IN THE GRECO-ROMAN WORLD

Gail Paterson Corrington
Rhodes College

ABSTRACT

In the medical, philosophical, and theological discourse of the early Christian period (first to fourth centuries CE), there is a link made between control of one bodily appetite (eating) and another (sex). That there is a connection between the sexual appetite and the appetite for bodily nourishment is summarized already by Soranus, the Greek medical writer, in the second century. He uses the metaphor of one appetite—eating—for another—sex. While, as Michel Foucault has noted in *The Care of the Self*, there seems to have been a much greater emphasis in Roman medical and philosophical writers on the "alimentary regimen" (140–141) than on sexual satisfaction and its control, the two are consistently linked and have become even more so in early Christian writings of both men and women. The language of the appetite becomes a means of asserting the boundaries of the person (a "self") and thereby asserting or recovering one's autonomy over against "outside" (heteronomous) forces. The strategy of this discourse is thus to define control over the self by defining what enters it (in the case of women) or leaves it (in the case of men). Anxiety over lack or loss of sexual control (being controlled by another "body" or person) is alleviated through the metaphorical assertion of control over what foreign substances ("bodies") may enter one's "own."

It is customary for scholars of early Christianity to locate the origin of the early Christians' expressed unease with the body in the division of body and soul that was supposedly well-established by the end of the classical period (Miles: 4). However, not all of the Greek and Roman writers, especially the medical "philosophers," were as concerned about the separation of the two as with their interaction. In their writings, they expressed the body as the sphere of operation of the spirit. As the metaphor of the "sphere" implies, the body was therefore spoken of as an integrity, a unit whose substance and spirit were subject either to diminution and loss, or to invasion and penetration. Galen, for example, revived in the second century CE the teaching of Hippocrates on the unity of the body as a total organism in which faculties or powers (*dynameis*) function to produce various changes or "alterations" (Brock: ix-xi).

The Epicurean and Stoic philosophers, no less concerned with the "care of the self," as Foucault has it (240), adopted the medical language about the interaction of body and soul or spirit. The Epicurean Roman poet and philosopher of the first century BCE, Lucretius, speaks of the identity of mind with spirit, and of their intertwining with the body as material entities (*De rer. nat.* III.126; 189). Like the body, the spirit or soul is capable of being "invaded" by disease (III.453) and "wounded" by desire (IV.1078). Moreover, from Lucretius' Epicurean point of view, the "vital spirit" or *animus*, is subject, in extreme pain and death, to diminution (III.257). The first century CE Roman Stoic writer and philosopher Seneca also expressed the "interweaving" of the body and soul as necessary to the care of one's own personal good (*hominis corpus animumque curantis, Ep. ad Lucil.* 66.45, cited by Foucault: 240). Hence, early Christian writers like Tertullian, when faced with the importance and value of the body implied in the two central Christian beliefs of Incarnation and Resurrection, had available the Greco-Roman medical and philosophical literature from which to find metaphors for the attunement of the body to the "movements of the spirit" within it (Brown: 77).

Yet this attunement of body to spirit was not inevitably seen as producing a harmony. Indeed, in Greek, Roman, and Christian writing, beginning in the fourth century BCE and continuing through the first four centuries of the Common Era and beyond, the establishment of balance and harmony between body and spirit is portrayed as a difficult art, with an increasing use of the discourse of "control." Exercise of control over the body and spirit, the two components of the "self," also became a symbolic way of exerting control over the relationships between the self and others, particularly those others like women, children and slaves, who could be seen as "bodies" and objects of control. Thus, as Foucault notes, the meaning of "*sōma*" or "body" was extended from the realm of the individual self to that of one's "possessions" in general (27). The most obvious and elementary form of control was that exercised over the sexual act, which for the male was described as the transmission of some of his "substance" (*ousia*) to another, entailing a truly material loss. Lucretius warned against the "tyrannical lust" caused by "that drop of Venus' honey that first drips into our heart," occasioning in men the desire to "transmit something of one's own substance from body to body" (*De rer. nat.* IV.1078). Lucretius observed a similar occurrence in attacks of epilepsy: an *expulsion* of vital spirit (III.522) because of the "invasion" of the body by "the contagion of disease" (III.453). In both cases—the sex-act and the epileptic seizure—that which is taken *in* is described as causing a corresponding *loss* or diminution of bodily "substance" or "spirit." Both are also perceived as losses of a vital component of the male "self," the substance that is also spoken of as "spirit": that is, sperm.

It is also important to observe in this context that Lucretius chooses as a metaphor for sexual desire a type of food, a substance that enters the body: "Venus' honey" occasions the "wound" of desire that enters a man and robs him of his "substance." The man is thus "penetrated," and loses an essential part of his manhood, thereby being diminished as a man and hence more "womanish." The use of the metaphor of food for sexual desire, and the connection between feeding and the sex-act are by no means peculiar to the discourse of the Epicureans. Indeed, as Galen observed, both the sex-act, which is spoken of as *genesis*, the act of conception, and also nutrition, the intake of nutriment by various organs of the body, are modes of alteration of the organism (*Nat. fac.* I.v). Hence, what Foucault describes as the "preoccuption with diet" in Greco-Roman medical writing (141). This sense of "preoccupation" results from the tendency of the writers to describe any alterations in the body in similar terms, so that "eating" becomes a metaphor for the sex-act (particularly as it views the woman as the "receiver" of the male sperm). Control of the diet itself therefore becomes a means of controlling intercourse. As Aline Rousselle notes, the object of controlling their diet and mode of living, for Greek and Roman men, was not only to produce an heir by facilitating the retention of seminal fluid (*pneuma* as sperm), but also to prevent the "draining" of their "vital spirit" (*pneuma* as the breath that is mixed with the seminal fluid) through too-frequent sexual activity (19).

While Greek and Roman males are urged to defend their bodies carefully against this deleterious draining off of their vital spirit, their medical advisors were also of the opinion that women's bodies needed to be controlled, to prevent them from being open to any "unseasonable" intercourse that would result not only in their draining of male *pneuma*, but also in the invasion or penetration of their own bodies by an illegitimate possessor or inappropriate power. In this type of discourse, the metaphor of eating is used for the act of intercourse. The woman's body, like the stomach, is described as capable of being "filled." As Page du Bois has observed, both Greek and Roman male writers used metaphors like "vase" and "field" to describe women's bodies as "receptacles" for male seed (184–88). Moreover, although the classical writers generally agreed that women produced a type of sperm, Aristotle concluded that it was "imperfect," lacking one important ingredient, "the principle of soul" (*De gen. animal.* 737a25). Thus, while men gave out or "lost" their vital spirit in the sex-act, women took in or received it. Galen also observed that male sperm was *active*, while female sperm was *acted upon* (*Nat. fac.* II.iii).

In their medico-philosophical speculations about the female body, moreover, both Soranus of Ephesus in the first half of the second century CE and Galen in the second half, spoke of a similarity in function or faculty between the stomach and the uterus. Soranus, in his manual on *Gynaecology*, which was written for men, contended that the best time for a woman to have intercourse resulting in conception was after her menstrual period, since the uterus, as an "avid" organ with an "appetite" of its own, would not ingest one nutriment (sperm) if it were full of another (blood) (*Gynaec.* I.10). Moreover, he cautioned that the uterus of a pregnant woman should not be shaken up by intercourse in the early stages of pregnancy, lest it "vomit up" the seed as the shaken stomach vomits food (I.14). Galen observed that both the stomach and the uterus exhibit the natural "faculty" of "retention" (*Nat. fac.* III.ii). Like Soranus, he advises intercourse for conception immediately after the cessation of the menstrual flow, so that the uterus, "empty" of blood but still warm enough for the "cooking" process perceived as necessary to conception, will "crave" sperm (Galen in Oribasius, *Corpus Medicorum Graecorum* XXII.7). Rufus of Ephesus, writing at the beginning at the second century CE, further recommends that a woman take a "less invigorating" diet than her spouse, if she is preparing to "receive" his sperm (Rufus in Orib., *CMG* I.594ff.). Thus, we may conclude that the "emptiness" of the womb was perceived as a necessary condition for its reception of "nutriment," and that the uterus and the stomach alike were described as ingesting a kind of "food," active in their craving of it, but passive in their receiving it.

Yet another aspect of the male definition of the female body as an "empty" receptacle for spirit, and its perceived capability to be entered or penetrated, is illustrated by Rudolph Arbesmann, in his study of the importance of fasting in prophetic discourse in antiquity. Arbesmann notes that, especially for mantic or magical activity, ritual purity (*hagneia*) was "required in preparation for magical intercourse with supernatural forces" (7). He attributes ritual fasting like that practiced for the Thesmophoria, a festival of Demeter open only to married women, to the belief that in "the act of taking food, . . demonic forces could use this opportunity to enter the human body and produce destructive effects" (6). He also confirms as typical the view of antiquity that a woman's body needs to be "empty," both of food and of evil spirits, the latter perhaps even *taken in* in the very act of ingestion, so that it can be "filled" with the good spirits of fertility, and prepared for the receipt of the male spirit/sperm (11). Moreover, although both men and women prophets in antiquity are described as fasting in order to prepare for the reception of spirits, it was the opinion of the ancients that women were more "open" to this particular "invasion of the divine" and especially to the ecstatic type of possession or *enthousiasmos* ("having the god within") that was frequently described in terms of sexual "penetration" of the female body (10; Corrington: 52). In this act of spiritual intercourse, an analogue to the biological and social act of sexual intercourse, the woman was spoken of as the receptacle of the "spirit" of her divine "possessor," just as she was seen as the receptacle of the "spirit" or "seed" of her human male "possessor."

At this point, we need to summarize briefly the Greco-Roman medical and philosophical discourse about the interaction between body and spirit, focusing particularly on the correspondence between discourse on the appetites for food and sex, before examining the adoption and modification of this discourse by early Christian ascetic writers. First, the classical writers described body and spirit as an interrelated unity, the body being the "sphere of operation" of the spirit. Second, the spirit is perceived as being equally affected by the body and may itself affect bodily alterations, primarily through controlling the two major means of alteration of the body, nutrition and sexual intercourse. In the case of men, control of ingestion of food assists in self-control by controlling the sex-act, through regulation of the production and expenditure of *pneuma*. In the case of women, ingestion of food by the stomach is a process compared to the ingestion of sperm by the uterus. In both forms of ingestion, which are also analogues of the "taking in" of a possessing spirit by a mantic, something is perceived as *entering* the woman's body, an organism portrayed as especially vulnerable to penetration, rather than something perceived as going *out* of it, as in the expenditure of a man's "spirit." Moreover, as Rousselle notes, the observations of women's bodies by physicians and philosophers, erroneous though they may have been, "helped men to take possession of the female body," extending their control of their own bodies to those bodies they socially and legally "possessed" (22). The defense of the male body thus was aimed at preventing loss of control by preventing loss of male "substance." That of the female body was aimed at protecting it from unwarranted invasion from the outside.

In the writings of the early Christian desert monastics, the struggle to maintain the proper control of body and spirit also was defined in terms of ingestion. As both Aline Rousselle and Peter Brown observe, "dietary privation remained the principal weapon in the fight against sexual desire" (Rousselle: 170–171; Brown: 217–218). The discourse of dietary regulation therefore becomes the discourse of control of desire. The most famous exponent of the desert ascetic mode of life, Anthony, is quoted as saying that "cramming" the body with food and drink causes the sex-organs, due to their proximity to the organs of digestion, to attempt to discharge the excess amounts of heat and energy generated by the excess of nutriment through sexual activity (Anthony, Saying 22, *Sayings of the Desert Fathers*). Phocas, another desert father, relates how Abba James was delivered from the "demon of fornication" by fasting for 40 days (Phocas, Saying 2, *SDF*). Both Tertullian (*De ieiun.* 5.1) and later Jerome (*Ep.* 54.9) quote Galen's advice on the reduction of sexual desire by fasting, while Clement of Alexandria advises women in particular to avoid eating too much food since "the redundance [i.e., of nutriment] flowing to the *pudenda*" arouses sexual desire (*Paed.* III.xi).

From these writings we may see that many of the early Christian writers, like their Greek and Roman antecedents, were concerned with the prevention of nocturnal emission or sexual activity, the consequence of which was the unregulated loss of their male "substance" (cf. Porphyry, *Ad Marcellam* 33), and whose cause they defined as over-indulgence in food and drink. They were no less concerned with the control of women's bodies and the regulation of the exercise of female sexuality. As for men, even more so for women, the "filling" of the body with food was viewed both as prelude and analogue to its "filling" with spirit, a spirit that might be "impure." The regulation of women's appetites, then, no less than of their own, became a preoccupation of early Christian male authors. As Rousselle notes:

> In this context [i.e., the early Christian], the pagan experiments with sexual abstinence and the sexual conditions which prevented women from giving free expression to their sexuality paved the way for Christian asceticism, and even in a sense led to its emergence as an alternative to hysteria. (131)

Thus, the avoidance of food by women could be perceived as a means of re-defining gender, of symbolically "becoming male" (137). Parallels between female fasting in antiquity and the modern phenomenon clinically named *anorexia nervosa* should be drawn with some care, but it may nevertheless be observed in this context that by means of severe fasting the female body may literally be on its way to becoming "male," or at least to becoming less obviously female by the erasure of female secondary sexual characteristics (Corrington: 53).

What little we have of the writing or recorded utterances of the church mothers, especially of the desert mothers, seems to indicate that their own discourse was not as preoccupied with fasting as was that of the fathers. Syncletica (*Apoph. Patr.* PG 65.424D), as Herbert Musurillo notes, urges "fasting and prayer as a cure for evil thoughts," but, like Julian of Norwich, prefers sickness as a more appropriate vehicle for the expression of female *askēsis* (31). Amma Theodora, when questioned by some monks as to the best way to get rid of demons, prescribes, not the time-honored "cures" of fasting and prayer, but "humility" alone as the sovereign remedy (Theodora, Saying 6, *Apoph. Patr.*; PG 65.204A-B). Amma Sarah conquers her own "demon of fornication" through prayer (Sarah, Saying 2, *Apoph. Patr.*).

On the other hand, exceptional, even extreme and punitive fasting is commended to Christian women by their male advisors, and heroic examples of "fasting women" are held up for emulation by other Christians, especially virgins. Basil of Ancyra, a former physician, gives typical Greco-Roman medical advice to virgins on the deleterious impact of food upon sexual desire: "As the body grows fat it is inordinately stimulated by the sexual humors seething deep down, and it is goaded and driven on to sexual intercourse (*De vera virg. integ.* 6; PG 30.681C). John Chrysostom holds up the example of "the female ascetics who even at a tender age go without food or sleep" (*De stud. praesen.* 3; PG 63.488f), and commends Olympias for "tormenting" her body with fasting, specially mentioned among other "mortifications" (*Ep.* 8.4ff.). Athanasius speaks in a similar manner to consecrated virgins in his *Treatise on Virginity* 6–7: fasting "cures desire, dries up the body's humors, puts demons to flight, gets rid of evil thoughts."

Judging from these and other examples, we cannot assume that Christian women followed the advice of the fathers, internalizing the responsibility, assigned them by men, for the appetitive sins of gluttony and sexual temptation that drove the first couple out of Paradise (cf. Basil of Caesarea, *De ieiun. hom.* 1.4; PG 31.168B; Jerome, *Ep.* 22.10–11; PL 22.400–401). Indeed, as the examples from the desert mothers indicate, their discourse was not nearly as preoccupied with "control" of appetite as was that of the desert fathers. Brown, however, observes, perhaps judging from the numbers of fasting women used as examples in the sermons of Christian males, that "Women ascetics were famous for their ability to endure preternaturally long fasts," and attempts an explanation of why they developed this ability:

> Deprived of the clear boundary of the desert, their energies less drained by hard physical labor and unable to expose themselves far from their place of residence for fear of sexual violence, virgins frequently defined themselves as separate from the world through an exceptionally rigid control of their diet (236; cf. Bynum: 78–93).

Brown thus suggests that fasting and "control" of the diet among women were not merely acting out of the advice given them by their male spiritual mentors, nor acts of penance for the responsibility for sin assigned them by these same mentors, but may have been attempts at self-definition and self-control, the establishment of boundaries for a "self" that could not be penetrated. Once again, we may cautiously draw an analogy between this behavior and that modern form of behavior it so much resembles, and whose discourse borrows from the discourse of asceticism: *anorexia nervosa*. Modern anorectics, ninety-five per cent of whom are women, are described by themselves as well as by others as having a need to establish "absolute control" over their bodies and to protect their bodily integrity. They perceive this control and protection as afforded primarily through their refusal to "take in" food, but they also frequently identify this "taking in" with sexual penetration, as did the ancient medical writers (Corrington: 54). This repugnance towards bodily invasion is put most strikingly by a modern anorectic, "Henriette A.": "... the idea that there is something flowing into me, into my mouth or into the vagina, is maddening: *integer, integra, integrum* occurs to me—untouchable" (Thoma: 437–52).

We may gain yet another insight into the possible reasons ascetic women themselves may have had for fasting if we note that the female body was perceived in both the classical and early Christian world as particularly vulnerable to possession by spiritual "powers." As previously noted, both Arbesmann and Musurillo have observed that for the ancients fasting had the effect of banishing evil or demonic spirits (i.e., preventing their entry), as well as of inviting the "good spirits" to enter (Arbesmann: 6–10; Musurillo: 20–34). Perhaps the strenuous fasts of the ascetic Christian women, like their celibate lifestyle, were attempts to preserve the integrity of their bodies against "invasion" or "penetration" by an outside power. In support of this view, Arbesmann has shown that following the fast (*asitia*) of the prophetess of Apollo, certain foods or beverages were ingested as a prelude to the "entry" of the spirit of the god into her body (11–14). By extension, the lack of ingestion might be seen as preventing entrance.

Further evidence for the motives behind female fasting may be found in the scorn heaped upon the Montanist prophetesses Priscilla and Maximilla by their orthodox detractors. Hippolytus of Rome in particular mentions their food practices, accusing them of "novelties of fasts and feasts," including avoidance of all but the dry foods that were widely believed to "dry up" sexual humors (*Refut.* 8.12). The *Pseudo-Clementine Homilies*, while in one homily (9.10) recommending fasting as a means of "banishing evil spirits," find in another (3.23) that female prophecy "steals" the "seeds of the male." Why, if such behavior was widely commended in male discourse as a means of "control" when exercised by men over women or by women following the advice of men, would this behavior be condemned when practiced by women by their own volition? Perhaps the Montanist prophetesses were indeed following the standard medico-philosophical and religious advice of the day in order to protect their bodies from the invasion of evil spirits and to preserve them for the entry of good spirits, prophecy, and visions. Perhaps also the orthodox writers, like some medical authorities of our own day, resented women's appropriation of their "advice" in order to exert control over their own bodies, resisting penetration, invasion, and control from the "outside." For ascetic Christian men, fasting was seen as defending the integrity of the "self" by preventing sexual arousal and an inappropriate "expense of spirit in a waste of shame" (Shakespeare, *Sonnet* 129), a "loss of substance" expressing the forfeiture of bodily integrity. For ascetic women, fasting may have helped to define a "self" normally not accustomed to drawing its own boundaries, and to maintain its integrity as a unity of body and spirit by the refusal to "ingest" anything from the outside that would result in being controlled by another.

Summary Conclusion

The discourse of appetite thus provides a "body language" through which the self may be defined and its integrity protected. Metaphors of eating and drinking (ingestion) are used in order to provide a means of asserting control over the boundaries of the person. Through the expressed "control" of the appetite, the person "controls" his or her own self. Connecting the appetite for food with the sexual appetite is a strategy for providing for the defense of personal integrity from a perceived violation or transgression, a means of defending the person as a body from the assertions of other bodies. Anxiety over the inability to direct and to control sexual urges (one's own or another's) thus becomes translated into anxiety over ingestion of "foreign" substances (other bodies). The strategy developed here, by demonstrating how one bodily appetite may be controlled, is to alleviate fear of "loss of control" in the other, and to assert or reassert autonomy metaphorically.

WORKS CONSULTED

Apophthegmata Patrum
    1975   *The Sayings of the Desert Fathers.* Trans. Benedicta Ward. London: Mowbrays.

Arbesmann, Rudolph
    1949–51   "Fasting and Prophecy in Pagan and Christian Antiquity," *Traditio* 7:1–71.

Brown, Peter
    1988   *The Body and Society: Men, Women, and Sexual Renunciation in Early Christianity.* New York: Columbia University Press.

Bynum, Caroline Walker
   1987   *Holy Fast and Holy Feast: The Significance of Food to Medieval Women*. Berkeley: University of California Press.

Corrington, Gail Paterson
   1986   "Anorexia, Asceticism, and Autonomy," *JFSR* 2.2: 51–63.

du Bois, Page
   1988   *Sowing the Body*. Chicago: University of Chicago Press.

Foucault, Michel
   1988   *History of Sexuality III: The Care of the Self*. Trans. Robert Hurley. New York: Random House.

Galen
   1928   *Galen, On the Natural Faculties*. Trans. by Arthur John Brock. LCL. New York: Putnam.

Lucretius
   1962   *Lucretius, On the Nature of the Universe*. Trans. R. E. Latham. Baltimore: Penguin.

Miles, Margaret R.
   1979   *Augustine on the Body*. AARDS 31. Missoula, MT: Scholars Press.

Musurillo, Herbert
   1956   "The Problem of Ascetical Fasting in the Greek Patristic Writers," *Traditio* 12:1–64.

Oribasius
   1928–33   *Corpus Medicorum Graecorum (CMG)*. Ed. J. Raeder. (Citation from Rouselle, q.v.)

Rouselle, Aline
   1988   *Porneia: On Desire and the Body in Antiquity*. Trans. by Felicia Pheasant. Oxford: Basil Blackwell.

Thoma, Helmut
   1977   "On the Psychotherapy of Patients with Anorexia Nervosa," *Bull. Meninger Clinic* 41: 437–52.

II

ASCETICISM AND IDEOLOGY:
THE LANGUAGE OF POWER IN THE PASTORAL EPISTLES

Lucinda A. Brown
Claremont Graduate School

ABSTRACT

The use of language reflects the ways in which power is exercised within a community, as well as the status and roles on which claims to power are based. The language of the Pastoral Epistles and its underlying ideological assumptions are examined here through an analysis of the experiential, relational, and expressive values of the text's lexical and grammatical systems, larger-scale structures, and interactional conventions. Particular attention is given to the use of ascetic language, including the use of catalogues of vices and virtues and the genderization of virtues, as a means of establishing social roles within the community and defining the parameters of the legitimate exercise of authority.

I. Introduction

The Pastoral Epistles have long been a source of numerous problems with which New Testament scholars have had to wrestle. Who authored the Pastorals? Who were the "opponents," and what had they done to attract the author's attention? What characteristics of the lifestyle and developing organization of the early church were reflected? The list of questions that attempt to place the Pastorals in their historical, ecclesiastical, and theological contexts is quite lengthy.

While much has been written on questions regarding dating, authorship, literary sources, and the like, somewhat less attention has been devoted to the question of what the Pastorals tell us about the social formation of the community to which they were addressed. Of particular interest here are the ways in which the Pastorals as discourse reflect the exercise of power and its impact on the development of social roles within the community.

Donelson and others have noted a strong dualism running through the Pastorals. The texts indeed at first appear to have been structured along lines of distinction drawn between sound doctrine and false teaching, between adherence to tradition and "falling away," and between virtues and vices.

Of particular interest here is an apparent distinction between church leaders who, on the basis of the authority granted them by tradition, could legitimately speak and act for the church, and others who could not so speak and act on behalf of the church because they had not been granted the authority to do so. Those who presumed to speak or act beyond what was allowed by their assigned role are derided in the Pastorals. Later commentators have perpetuated this understanding by categorically describing such persons as, e.g., "unattached busybodies" (Donelson: 117).

Donelson has observed further that many studies of the Pastoral Epistles, particularly studies of the so-called opponents, have not taken the creativity of the author seriously and that the characterizations of Timothy's opponents were, in fact, paradigmatic of the author's own opponents (118). The concern here is not with linking the opponents with any particular group in the history of early Christianity. The concern is rather one of process: an examination of the Pastoral Epistles as units of discourse is a means of revealing the ways in which the points of tension reflected the social relationships within one early Christian community, as well as the ways in which the language of right doctrine and right practice reflected the exercise of power by one group over another.

II. Language and Power

Drawing on the work of Berger and Luckmann, the following analysis assumes that human experiences must be continually objectivated in order to be understood meaningfully. Experiences must be organized into larger, integrative schemas which are mutually understood by both producers and receivers of the products of human activity. Such organization is accomplished through the human production of signs, of which language is assumed to be one of the most crucial.

Language is not only a means by which knowledge is constructed and organized. The use of language " ... constitutes the statuses and roles upon which people base their claims to exercise power, and the statuses and roles which seem to require subservience" (Fowler: 61–62). In short, discourse is social practice determined by social structures. Actual discourse is determined by sets of conventions associated with social institutions, while orders of discourses are ideologically shaped by power relationships in social institutions and societies.

Power relationships are themselves socially constructed realities. They represent the " ... process whereby social groupings with different interests engage with one another" (Fairclough: 34). Power is reflected in discourse by the constraint and control over contents, relations, and subject positions placed by certain participants (the powerful) over the contributions of others (the non-powerful). Fairclough argues that the social order of discourse is constructed and maintained by the "hidden effect of power" (55) and, indeed, that ideology " . . . is most effective when its workings are least visible" (85). Invisibility is achieved when a particular ideological stance is embedded within a set of assumptions rather than made an explicit element of a text. Ideological power is thus exercised when the powerful are able to project their own practices as universal and commonsensical. Through the signification process, a text can thus position its hearers in such a way that a particular ideological stance can be brought to the text's interpretation and then reproduced through the interpretive process.

Fairclough offers a model which attempts to uncover the power relationships underlying the framework of a text, thereby exposing the text's ideological assumptions. Key elements of the model include the experiential, relational, and expressive values of a text's lexical and grammatical systems, as well as the text's larger-scale structures and interactional conventions. The model allows for the examination of a variety of features, including the use of classification schemes, euphemistic expressions, nominalizations, pronouns, logical connectors, and modes of coordination/subordination in complex sentences.

III. The Pastoral Epistles: An Examination of the Language of Power

The immediate concern is to examine the structure and use of language in the Pastoral Epistles. A linguistic analysis can further the understanding of the social relationships within the community to which the Pastorals were addressed, as well as reveal the ways in which the community's leaders utilized the language of orthodoxy and orthopraxy to establish a particular ideological position.

(a) Rhetorical Strategy

The author's rhetorical strategy appears to have been motivated largely by issues internal to the community being addressed. The intent would not necessarily have been to persuade non-believers of the efficacy of adopting the author's belief system. Rather, the arguments presented would have served to support a particular set of ideas about social roles and the relationships between church leaders and others within the community.

The arguments in the Pastorals were deliberative in nature and were concerned with concrete decisions and courses of action within the life of the community. But while Aristotelian deliberative rhetoric drew on the state and on the role of virtue in the public life as a model, the rhetorical strategy here drew instead on God's plan of salvation, the perceived needs of the church, and the role of virtue in both public and private life (Donelson: 80). The special topics contained herein derived from specific salvation statements, entrusted traditions, and the community's mutually agreed upon concept of the religious life.

(b) Discourse Analysis: The Lexical System

Lists of Vices and Virtues

The lists of vices and virtues appear to have been a key classificatory device in the Pastorals. More extensive study would be required to determine whether any set criteria, such as number of items per list and internal logic, existed in antiquity for the compilation of such lists, as well as to determine more precisely the nature of the relationships between specific vices and virtues. Further study would also be required to understand the lists found in the Pastorals more fully in comparison to lists found in other writings of the period.

A cursory examination reveals that the lists in the Pastorals varied both in length and in the issues addressed. Relatively short lists are found, e.g. in 1 Timothy 1:13, describing Paul's former life as a blasphemer, persecutor, and violent person, and 1 Timothy 4:12, listing the ways in which Timothy was to serve as a model for believers. Longer lists are found in 1 Timothy 1:9–10, listing the persons for whom the law was given; 1 Timothy 3:1–7 and Titus 1:7–9, listing the characteristics of bishops; 1 Timothy 3:8–10 and 12–13, listing the characteristics of deacons; 1 Timothy 5:3–16, listing the characteristics of widows; 2 Timothy 3:1–5, listing the characteristics of the last days; and Titus 2:2–10, listing the characteristics of various groups within the community—older and younger men, older and younger women, and slaves.

A key issue has to do with what can be said about the functions of such lists. Donelson has suggested that the lists in the Pastorals served three basic functions—apologetic, polemical, and paideutic (173–76). Such an understanding of the lists in the Pastorals is not without its problems. It is true, as Donelson has noted, that, superficially, the lists of vices and virtues in the Pastorals contained nothing with which non-Christians of the period could not agree (10). Certain components of the lists, such as *sōphrosynē*, appeared in both Christian and non-Christian writings of the period. Yet the larger texts within which the lists were embedded were not addressed to a non-Christian audience, nor was the apparent intent the legitimation of Christian values to non-believers in the face of a hostile non-Christian environment. While it is true that the Pastorals demonstrated a concern for maintaining cordial relations with outsiders, the extent to which they were addressed to believers who intentionally threatened that cordiality is not clear. It is not immediately evident, therefore, that the lists served any particular apologetic function.

Considering the rhetorical strategy of the author, it is more likely that the lists served polemical and paideutic functions, to bolster an already prevalent social hierarchy of roles and strengthen the ties between that hierarchy and emerging Christian ideals. The vice lists found in 1 Timothy 1:9–10 and 2 Timothy 3:1–5 are the most polemical of all the lists contained in the Pastorals. According to Donelson, Dibelius and Conzelmann rightly caution against linking the items in these lists too closely with actual persons and events in the community, arguing instead that the lists were "... intended to have the effect of posters" (23). Similar lists found in *The Shepherd of Hermas*, John Chrysostom's *Baptismal Instructions*, and other Christian writings indicate that throughout Christian antiquity it was not uncommon for authors to fire off in rapid succession a number of undesirable conditions and actions, including conditions and actions found in the Pastorals' vice lists. Indeed, the adulterer, the fornicator, and the drunkard, among others, appear to have been well-known stereotypical personages in early Christian writings. The length of the lists found in the Pastorals, combined with the alliteration and assonance produced by the appropriate placement of particular terms, would surely have served as an attention-getting device, as well as a means of continually reminding the audience that behaviors which undermined the prevailing social order were unacceptable.

Indeed, the common framework which bound these otherwise disparate behaviors together was precisely that they had all come to represent a loss of self-control. The repeated use of body-related images would have struck a chord in bourgeois Greco-Roman culture, serving to underscore the undesirability of the disorder occasioned by the loss of control. In the Pastorals, as elsewhere, the vice lists included activities such as drunkenness and engagement in socially unacceptable sexual behavior as symbols of that which the audience was to avoid. It is worth noting that the semantic domain for sexual terminology in antiquity appears to have been quite different from that of later centuries. Scholars are rightly cautioned against reading contemporary understandings and biases into the vice and virtue terminology of antiquity. Thus, e.g., *arsenokoitas* may well have connoted male prostitution throughout antiquity, as Boswell has suggested, rather than homosexuality or sodomy (107).

In short, the body images served as metaphors for the social unit. Individual dysfunctional behavior would have been symbolic of dysfunctional behavior on the part of the community as a whole. Similar images, such as the image of drunkenness, functioned in a similar manner elsewhere in the Pastorals. The author did not advocate total abstinence; he advised "Timothy" at one point to "drink a little wine for the stomach and your frequent afflictions" (1 Tim 5:23). According to the lists describing bishops and deacons, however, these church officers were not to be drunkards (1 Tim 3:1–5), and were not to partake of much wine (1 Tim 3:8–10). The concern clearly had to do with moderation. Other components of the vice and virtue lists advocating order and self-control included the designation of bishops and deacons as good managers of their households and as men who were able to maintain order and discipline among their wives and children.

In their polemical attack against those who did not live the "religious life" (as defined by the author), the vice lists here appear to have served as a negative reinforcement of a prevailing set of ideas about social roles. The identity of those who adhered to sound doctrine and right practice would have been marked off in stark contrast to those who were described as lawless and insubordinate, the former being those who maintained social order, the latter being those whose actions led to social chaos.

Of the functions proposed by Donelson, the paideutic is argued to have been the one most evident in the lists in the Pastorals. The function is evidenced most clearly in the various lists of characteristics of church officers and other groups within the Christian community. The virtues and vices already familiar from other literature of the Greco-Roman period are discovered most readily in these lists. These lists also provide not only an indication of the kind of behavior the audience was to avoid, but also the kind of behavior the audience was to emulate. The use of vice and virtue lists as an instructional device in the religious life was not unique to the Pastorals. Such use is found at least as late as Basil, whose *Discourse on Ascetical Discipline* included a list describing the characteristics of the ideal monk. Like the bishops and deacons described in the Pastorals, Basil's monk was, among other things, to maintain modesty of bearing, spend his time in good works and deeds, not swear, refrain from reveling and drunkenness, and have nothing to do with secular concerns.

The lists of characteristics of different groups found in 1 Timothy 3:1–7, 3:8–10 and 12–13, 5:3–16, and Titus 1:7–9 demonstrate clearly the use of this classificatory device to differentiate between social relationships within the community. As with the vice lists, the author here fired off in rapid succession the characteristics of those who aspired to be bishops and deacons, although the lists were not similarly distinguished by the use of assonance and alliteration. The lists were distinguished by the emphasis placed on the maintenance of order and self-control: church officers were to be sound-minded, temperate, not addicted to much wine, not violent, able to govern household and family well, and so forth.

Some of these characteristics were mentioned in the Pastorals in passages other than the vice and virtue lists. In 2 Timothy 1:7, for example, the author reminded "Timothy" that God gave "to us" a spirit of "power and love and soundmindedness," thus placing *sōphrosynē* in a Christian context. What is not clear is whether, by referring to such virtues in a seemingly general context, the author intended to obscure the distinctions between church officers and the general membership. If so, then the purpose of using such extensive lists to describe bishops and deacons as distinct groups would have to be questioned. The extent to which bishops and deacons had emerged within the early church as distinct offices at this point in time is not clear, and it may be that they were presented here simply as models which the entire Christian community was to emulate. In such a case, however, the distinction between church leaders and the general membership would have been obscured and claims such as that found in 1 Timothy 3:1 would have been meaningless.

An alternative solution is suggested here, namely, that the Pastorals were addressed to those who already served the church in positions of authority, so that when the author wrote " . . . God did not give *to us* a spirit of timidity, but of power and love and soundmindedness," he was referring only to church leaders and not to the membership at large. In keeping with the notion that Timothy's opponents were paradigmatic of the author's own opponents, this solution would likewise maintain that the author, and Timothy and Titus, were paradigmatic of the early church leadership. The language of vice and virtue would thus have served here an instructional function in the training of early church leaders.

Vices and Virtues: A Gender-Based Understanding

The list in 1 Timothy 5:3–16 describing the characteristics of those who aspired to be "real" widows stands in stark contrast to the lists describing bishops and deacons. An immediate concern was the distinction between those who were to be enrolled as "real" widows and those who were not. Distinctions between "real" and "false" bishops and "real" and "false" deacons were not found in the corresponding lists. Further, in addition to the renewed use of assonance as a means of emphasis, the characteristics listed no longer described activity concurrent with the assumption of the role, but actions or conditions that were to have been achieved prior to assuming the role. Thus, for example, while bishops were to be hospitable (*philoxenon* governed by the present infinitive *einai*), a woman must have already shown hospitality (*xenodoxēsen* governed by *ei*) in order to qualify as a "real" widow.

Further study is needed to determine the significance of the use of different terms denoting the practice of hospitality by male and female church officers. Liddell and Scott distinguish between the two terms and argue that *philonene* and its correlates are defined in a general way as being hospitable, while *xenodochas* and its correlates appear to be defined more specifically in terms of receiving or hosting strangers and guests. Liddell and Scott define *to xenodixeion* as a place for strangers to lodge, i.e., an inn. Lampe defines the same term as a guest-house or hospice for travellers, the sick, and the poor. The association of the widows with such an institution would certainly be in keeping with the requirement that they be known for their good works. Lampe further defines *xenodocheō* not only in terms of serving as a host or hostess, but also as a guestmaster in a church or monastery. Later attestations of the term thus took on the connotation of a church officer who performed particular duties, as distinct from a more general hospitable nature. Most of the other New Testament attestations of the practice of hospitality rely on *philonene* and its correlates (Rom 12:13, Titus 1:8, Heb 13:2, and 1 Pet 4:9). On the other hand, James 2:25 uses *upodeamenē* in describing Rahab's reception of the spies. Whether or not there is a connection between this term and that which was expected of the widows remains to be determined. It is, however, suggestive in light of the tradition that remembered Rahab's hospitality, as well as the tradition found in Josephus and in later Jewish writings that obscured Rahab's role as a prostitute and remembered her instead as an innkeeper. In any case, it perhaps can be speculated that the widows of 1 Timothy 5 might have been expected to have performed particular hospitable duties not required of their male counterparts.

Similarly, a bishop was to be generous, not greedy, righteous, and pious, while a "real" widow must have demonstrated that she had already fulfilled certain requirements, such as having reached a certain age, having washed the feet of the saints, assisted the afflicted, and been devoted to good works, before she could assume the role. Even a cursory examination of the vice and virtue lists reveals a gender differential in the way in which male and female church roles were assigned and described.

Foucault and others have already noted the gender-based understanding of vices and virtues in Greco-Roman antiquity, arguing that the same term could mean one thing when applied to men and something quite different when applied to women. *Sōphrosynē*, for example, typically denoted moderation, mastery, and self-control when applied to men, and chastity when applied to women. Foucault noted not only the gender-based difference in the application of this virtue, but also the extent to which the virtue represented the social roles which men and women were to assume (78–86). Such an understanding was reinforced here not only through different requirements for assuming certain roles within the community, but also through the increased specificity with which women were instructed, as in 1 Timothy 2:10, where women were instructed as to apparel appropriate for them to wear (no gold, no pearls, no expensive clothing, and no braided hair). Nowhere in the Pastorals were men instructed in such detail, particularly with regard to their physical appearance.

Gender-based differences were linked in the Pastorals to the issue of authority and to distinctions between church officers and general members. This connection is most apparent in 1 Timothy 5:11–15, where young widows are derided for engaging in what is described as idle behavior, excessive visitation, gossip, and officiousness. The charge against the young widows is followed immediately by the instruction that they are to marry, rear children, and manage the household, i.e. assume the traditional role for women of child-bearing age. It is argued here that the negative description of the young widows may have had less to do with any actual idle or officious behavior on their part than it did with the attempt of the male-dominated hierarchy to regulate female activity and to suppress efforts by female members of the congregation to expand the scope of their authority.

The charges against the younger widows are included in the larger discussion of the role of widows in the community. The description of widows in 1 Timothy 5:3–16 represented a restricting of the arena in which a certain group of women participated and a limiting of the corporate power of that group. While allowing that "real widows" were to be honored, the author narrowly defined a "real widow" as one who no longer had family to support her. Indeed, a "real widow" was not only one who had no children, but one who had no grandchildren to whom she could turn for support. In an age when the average lifespan of women was relatively short and many women would not have lived long enough to know their grandchildren, let alone be supported by them, the specification that a "real widow" have neither children nor grandchildren was, at the very least, rather odd. Those who could be known as "real widows" were further narrowly—and with some hyperbole—defined as those who were at least sixty years of age (at a time when many women would not have lived to such an age), who had been married to only one husband (at a time when, the ideal of *univira*, or being married to one man, aside, young widows were penalized under Augustan legislation for not remarrying), and who had already performed particular roles within the community (at a time when there was some tension, at least, with regard to women's public roles). The impact of the increasingly narrow definition of "real widow" would have been to separate women from one another who collectively might have wielded a certain degree of power within the community.

A "real widow" was also defined as one whose hope was set on God (presumably rather than on human institutions), and who devoted herself to prayer and supplication "night and day." A possible implication of the passage is that a "real widow," having met the requirements of age and means of support (or lack thereof), and having proven herself by her good works, would upon enrollment have devoted herself to a life of prayer. A "real widow" was by definition one who had been removed from the arena of public life in which she had previously participated.

Because of their age and probable familial ties, the young widows were also by definition unable to participate in the ideal of the "real widow" just described. By charging the young widows to marry, rear children, and manage households, the author was clearly attempting to diminish the possibility that those who were currently young widows would one day meet the requirements of a "real widow." The paradox was set: while the "real widow" was one who, having met the ideal of *univira*, had engaged publicly in good works and was now able to devote herself to God without distractions, the young widows were instructed to follow a course that would prevent them from ever being considered a "real widow." The young widows were not only segregated from the older women in whose tradition they might follow, they were also prevented from participating in the very piety for which the older widows had just been idealized.

In short, 1 Timothy 5:11–15 represented an attempt to keep women in their place by restricting the sphere of their activity and autonomy. The tension here had more to do with the *process* of defining roles within the community and with determining *who* could participate in the decision-making process, than it did with the actual content of the activity in which the young widows were participating. The role of the young widows was defined in such a way that public activity on their part was deemed inappropriate. Attempts by the young widows to continue their public activity—perhaps engaging in the tradition of good works, hospitality, washing the feet of the saints, and assisting the afflicted— were discredited as idle or officious behavior, or as a matter of the widows speaking what was not proper. The author closed his discreditation of the widows by stating that widows who were not supported by their families were a burden on the church, thus negating any positive contribution that the widows may have made to the life of the church.

Similar attempts occur elsewhere in the Pastorals. For example, in 1 Timothy 2:12, women are instructed that they are not to teach or assert themselves over men. While virtually every other New Testament attestation of the exercise of authority was expressed by some form of *exousia*, denoting authority that had been granted one by someone higher in the hierarchical schema, 1 Timothy 2:12 expressed the prohibition as *oude authentein*. It appears that women were not being forbidden the proper exercise of traditional authority which they might have expected to have been granted in the normal course of the community's life. Nor is there any evidence that the women of the community were exercising authority over their male counterparts, as Bauer and other lexicographers have suggested (Bauer: 120; Moulton: 91). Rather, assuming that *authentein* derives in part from *autoō*, it may be inferred that the term referred here to the assumption of authority on one's own part, as distinct from authority granted by another. Attestations of such usage are found in non-biblical writings, so that the use of *authentein* here to refer to the women's assumption of their own authority would not be without precedent (Lampe: 262). In such a case, it can be argued that the women of the community had been attempting to exercise authority which had not been specifically granted them by the male hierarchy, thereby expanding their scope of acceptable activity. In short, the women of the community had attempted to change the rules of the game. 1 Timothy 2:12 illustrates the exercise of power on the part of the male hierarchy to prevent such a change in the rules from occurring.

Admonition Regarding the Life of Piety

The vice and virtue lists highlighted the way of life the readers were to avoid, as well as the way of life they were to emulate. The message that the readers were to adhere to a particular lifestyle was reinforced by the repeated mention of that lifestyle throughout the entire discourse (1 Tim 1:5; 1:18–20; 2:1–4; 2:10; 3:14–15; 4:7–8; 4:12, 16; 6:6, 11, 13; 2 Tim 2:22–26; Titus 2:11–15; 3:1). The practice of the "right" ascetic life was further linked with "right" belief, the stated goal of each being the maintenance of a unifying communal system that would provide for a "tranquil and quiet life," i.e. a stable social order.

The importance of maintaining a stable social order based on a hierarchy of roles is evident both from the way in which the author described the "right" ascetic life and from the way in which the author referred to those who did not adhere to that life. The "right" ascetic life was referred to in military terms (e.g., fighting the good fight—1 Tim 1:18, 6:12; enduring as a good soldier of Christ—2 Tim 2:3–4) and in religious terms (e.g., living the holy, righteous, or pious life—1 Tim 4:7–8, 6:11; 2 Tim 2:16, 3:12, 16; Titus 2:12), while opponents were referred to as having erred or turned to idle disputation (1 Tim 1:6, 4:1), as having shipwrecked their faith (1 Tim 1:19), and as being conceited or not well-versed (1 Tim 6:4), and the life of the opponents as secular or one in which people were concerned with silly myths and endless genealogies that led to useless speculation (1 Tim 1:4). Thus the lifestyle and belief system advocated by the author were characterized in positive terms, associated with standard contemporary social structures with which the readers could readily identify, and supported by appeals to "the truth." The lifestyle and belief system of the opponents, on the other hand, were described as deviant, silly, useless, and without foundation (1 Tim 4:7, 6:3–5; 2 Tim 2:23; Tit 1:10–16, 3:9).

It is clear that the author was not advocating the ascetic life over and against a non-ascetic lifestyle. The author actively discouraged certain ascetic practices to which other Christians in the community may have been adhering. Withdrawal from the world, for example, was said to be inappropriate. Indeed, bishops were to have "good witness from outsiders" so as to prevent them from being entrapped by the devil (1 Tim 3:7). Abstinence from practices such as marriage and the eating of certain foods was also discouraged on the grounds that marriage and food were among God's good gifts and were to be enjoyed with thanksgiving by the faithful (1 Tim 4:1–6). But the author appears to be advocating a particular system of ascetic behavior that would support the effective ministry and public witness of the church. By encouraging adherence to the proper ascetic lifestyle among members of the church, Timothy, for example, is said to be "a good minister of Christ Jesus, being imbued with the words of faith and the good doctrine to which you have conformed" (1 Tim 4:6). The ascetic lifestyle advocated by the author also served to bolster the social hierarchy which had been established within this particular community. Throughout the Pastorals, those who maintained this hierarchy by assuming their proper social roles were described as adhering to the proper lifestyle, thus leading the life of faith (1 Tim 3:10, 13, 4:6; 2 Tim 1:13–14, 2:19, 21; Tit 1:7–9, 2:7–14). Those who did not keep their place, i.e. those who assumed some measure of autonomy and authority beyond that which had been assigned to them, were described as those who had adopted the incorrect lifestyle and who had fallen from the faith (1 Tim 1:6–7, 19–20, 4:1–3, 5:13, 6:20; 2 Tim 2:17–18, 3:2–9; Tit 1:10–16).

(c) Discourse Analysis: The Grammatical System

Experiential Features

Each of the Pastoral Epistles has been passed on in the form of instruction. The author, pseudepigraphically using the name of Paul, and the two named recipients, Timothy and Titus, represented the key participants and, as stated previously, are understood here as being paradigmatic. The situations described were personalized through references to individuals who did not play any apparent role in the text other than to help illustrate points made by the author (1 Tim 1:20, 2 Tim 1:16, 2:14, 2:15, 2:17, 4:19–22, and Tit 3:12–13). The appeal to Paul as the source of instruction strengthened the author's own position by placing the instruction squarely within a tradition that was widely known and was coming to be accepted as orthodox.

The instructions contained in the Pastorals were passed clearly from the author ("Paul") to the recipients named in the letters ("Timothy" and "Titus"), as is evidenced by the regular use of the first singular active and second singular imperative verbal forms. The vice and virtue lists are somewhat distinguished by their use of the impersonal *dei* followed by the present infinitive *einai* (1 Tim 3:2, 3:8, 3:11, and Tit 1:7). While the injunctions in the Pastorals tend to be stated positively, the vice and virtue lists, particularly those describing church officers, tend to be comprised of both positive and negative injunctions.

Relational Values

The author of the Pastorals relied principally on the declarative mode in stating his own desires and statements of intent, and the imperative mode in stating the behaviors which the readers were either to adopt or avoid. The texts are notably lacking in the use of questions. The use of declarative and imperative modes lends additional support to the notion that the rhetorical strategy here was to reinforce an already accepted structure of reality; questions, whether rhetorical or factual in nature, serve to persuade the readers to adopt a position with which they have not necessarily already fully agreed. The declarative and imperative modes here rely instead upon an assumed base of knowledge which is already shared by members of the audience.

The Pastorals are further personalized by the regular use of the second singular pronoun. The similarly regular use of indefinite pronouns in referring to the so-called opponents (1 Tim 1:3, 1:6, 1:8, 1:19, 2:1, 4:1, 6:1; 2 Tim 2:18; and Tit 1:10) and the infrequent use of the first plural pronoun (as in 1 Tim 2:2; 2 Tim 2:11; and Tit 2:11, 3:3) is striking. Such use of pronouns is consistent with the notion that the concern here was with distancing the author and his followers from a rival group (or groups) within the emerging Christian community.

The texts here are comprised of a mix of complex and simple grammatical structures. The doxological statements interspersing the texts (1 Tim 1:17, 2:5, and 3:16) tended to be fairly simple in construction. Other statements, e.g. 1 Tim 1:3–7, are convoluted to the point of being syntactically nonsensical. In only three instances in the Pastorals were thoughts interrupted by insertions (1 Tim 1:8–11, 2:5–7, and 6:11–16).

(d) Discourse Analysis: Textual Structure

The Pastorals are distinguished in part by the way in which one section leads to the next with virtually no logical connectors. Individual sections are constructed through the judicious use of certain connecting particles, with *de* being used more frequently than *kai* or *gar*. The rapid movement from one section to the next would have been an effective part of the author's rhetorical strategy, for the setting forth of the author's positions one after the other, with minimal accompanying argumentation or justification, would have elicited quick, presumably affirmative, responses on the part of the readers.

The movement back and forth between sections addressed specifically to "Timothy" or "Titus," and sections more general in nature, would have further bolstered audience response by appealing to that which was held to be universally known. The regular appeal to common sense is evident from a number of key phrases that appear throughout the Pastorals, including the *pistos ho logos* sayings (1 Tim 1:15, 3:1, 4:19; and 2 Tim 2:11) and the occasional appeals to what the readers were said to have already known (1 Tim 1:8; and 2 Tim 1:15, 3:14–15). "Truth" was thus something that was appealed to on the basis of shared experience, rather than the result of carefully articulated argumentation.

IV. The Language of Power and Social Formation in the Pastoral Epistles

Social formation is essentially a process of self-definition. As such, it is comprised of a number of components, including the development of social and leadership roles. Other components of the social formation process include code elaboration, boundary markers, distinguishing attitudes, practices and views, rituals, myths, and rites of entry and exclusion (Mack: 97). The Pastorals are distinguished by the extent to which many of these components are *not* explicitly elaborated. References to specific ritual practices, for example, are notably lacking, unless Titus 3:5 is understood to have been a reference to baptism. While a contrast is regularly made between those who adhered to the "religious life" and those who did not, nothing specific is said regarding the processes by which persons are admitted to or excluded from the community or participate together in the communal expression of the religious life.

The content of the community's belief system is also not fully elaborated. Both God and Christ are depicted, at different points, as agents of salvation. While the notion of universal salvation is clearly stated (1 Tim 2:3–4 and 4:10), a belief in the idea of God's elect is also present (2 Tim 2:8–10, 2:19–21; and Tit 1:4). God is further portrayed as the source of life and the giver of all good things. All that came from God is understood to be for human enjoyment. Indeed, this assertion is used as an argument against the apparent renunciations of some in the community against marriage and the eating of certain foods (1 Tim 4:1–6). Yet moderation appears to have been a key to the enjoyment of God's good gifts, for the author clearly identified excess as inappropriate behavior (1 Tim 6:6–10).

A belief in the unity, or oneness, of God also appears to have been key for this community. The author clearly stated that there was *one* God and *one* mediator between God and humanity (1 Tim 2:5). It was God who gave life to *all* things (1 Tim 6:13). God was the *only* sovereign who would reveal Christ's coming again (1 Tim 6:1–5). The oneness of God was linked with the universality of God's claim on humanity. Most important for our analysis here, the oneness of God was also linked with the notion of one absolute truth which believers were to accept. The tenets of this truth are never clearly articulated in the Pastorals. Indeed, whether or not the notion of truth represented a specific set of beliefs for this particular community cannot be argued on the basis of the texts as we have them. What can be said is that the idea of "truth" was linked further with the idea of the "religious life" and that both were used to distinguish between those who adhered to the author's position and those who did not. The monotheizing tendency, along with the idea of one truth, served as a means of social control, i.e. the maintenance of the existing hierarchy of social roles.

The Pastorals clearly set forth the community's internal schema of social roles as understood by the prevailing leadership. The author states that the Christian's holy calling and, indeed, salvation itself, were based on grace, not works (2 Tim 1:8–12; and Tit 3:1–8a). Those who were members of the author's community were thus presumably understood to be members of the community because of "grace." Yet the relationships of the various members of that community were clearly understood within the context of "works," where roles were distinguished on the bases of gender and age and were clearly not interchangeable.

The twin assertions that members of the community were justified by grace, but were also to engage in good works, supported the community's internal social system, which was constructed on the principle of dependence. Members of the community were dependent first upon God, whom community leaders pointed to as the source of life, the giver of all good things, and the one through whose mercy and grace they were justified (Tit 3:5–7). The "good life", i.e. life in God, could never be achieved by human initiative. Members of the community were further dependent upon their leaders, who determined the appropriate social and religious practice for the community, which, as Schüssler-Fiorenza has noted, resembled that of the Greco-Roman patriarchal household (289).

The posture of dependence was perpetuated by the repeated prohibitions against anything that might have distracted members of the community from living the "religious life," which was, as noted earlier, defined entirely by some of the community's leaders and represented by the author of the present texts. The audience was admonished not so much to avoid specific impious acts as it was to avoid "secular discussions" and "idle disputations" which may, in fact, have been nothing more than creative theologizing by those who were not in positions deemed appropriate for such activity.

V. Conclusion

In short, the Pastoral Epistles reflect the way in which one community understood the relationship between its internal social roles and its emerging self-definition. The preoccupation with leading a quiet and tranquil life and the use of virtues already well-known within the Greco-Roman world would certainly have minimized the extent to which this community was set apart from its Roman environment. The relative lack of conflict between the community and its larger social context would appear to be indicated by the absence of concern about specific rituals.

Indeed, the principal concern of the Pastorals appears to have been one of strengthening an emerging system of social roles within the community whereby only certain members of the community were allowed to assume positions of authority. Utilizing the language of the "religious life" to which members of the community were called, the author of the Pastorals distinguished the various social categories according to which the community was divided, and then discredited those who challenged him by their attempts to redefine the categories. The result was the solidifying of a hierarchical system in which the authority to make decisions regarding the community's beliefs and practices was based on predetermined roles rather than on the actual intellectual, spiritual, or organizational abilities of the persons who filled those roles. The social structure of this particular community was thus one in which authority was assumed only by those who filled roles at the top of the hierarchy, while those lower on the hierarchical ladder were not only denied access to that authority but were dismissed as trouble-makers when they challenged the system by which the community was structured.

The structuring of social roles was facilitated by the use of *sōphrosynē* as a principle virtue within the community. It is clear from the text itself that the community was familiar with more extreme forms of ascetic behavior (1 Tim 4:3), and that there were tensions within the community regarding the appropriate behavior of certain of its members (1 Tim 2:8, 11–12, 5:13, 6:2, 4–5; 2 Tim 2:14–17, 3:2–5; Tit 3:1). The piety which the community was called to practice, based as it was on moderation and self-control, served to mitigate the effects of the more extreme ascetic tendencies and to keep internal tensions in check. The life of moderation in turn served to strengthen the hierarchical social structure and to limit the creative exchange of ideas and sharing of power within the community.

WORKS CONSULTED

Berger, Peter L. and Luckmann, Thomas
    1966   *The Social Construction of Reality.* New York: Anchor.

Boswell, John
    1980   *Christianity, Social Tolerance, and Homosexuality.* Chicago: University of Chicago Press.

Dibelius, Martin, and Hans Conzelmann
    1972   *The Pastoral Epistles.* Philadelphia: Fortress.

Donelson, Lewis R.
    1986   *Pseudepigraphy and Ethical Argument in the Pastoral Epistles.* Tübingen: J. C. B. Mohr (Paul Siebeck).

Fairclough, Norman
    1989   *Language and Power.* London: Longman.

Foucault, Michel
    1985   *The History of Sexuality.* Vol. 2. *The Use of Pleasure.* Trans. Robert Hurley. New York: Vintage.

Fowler, Roger
    1985   "Power." Pp. 61–82 in *Handbook of Discourse Analysis.* Vol. 4. *Discourse Analysis in Society.* London: Academic.

Halliday, M. A. K.
    1973   *Explorations in the Functions of Language.* New York: Elsevier.
    1978   *Language as Social Semiotic: The Social Interpretation of Language and Meaning,* Baltimore: University Park.

Kress, Gunther
    1985   "Ideological Structure in Discourse." Pp. 27–42 in *Handbook of Discourse Analysis*. Vol. 4. *Discourse Analysis in Society*. London: Academic.

Lampe, G. W. H.
    1961   *A Patristic Greek Lexicon*. Oxford: Clarendon.

Liddell, Henry George, and Robert Scott
    1968   *A Greek-English Lexicon*. Revised with supplement. Oxford: Clarendon.

Mack, Burton L.
    1990   *Rhetoric and the New Testament*. Minneapolis: Fortress.

Moulton, James Hope and Milligan, George
    1930   *The Vocabulary of the Greek New Testament*. Grand Rapids: Eerdmans.

Schüssler Fiorenza, Elizabeth
    1983   *In Memory of Her*. New York: Crossroad.

THE LANGUAGE OF DESIRE:
CLEMENT OF ALEXANDRIA'S
TRANSFORMATION OF ASCETIC DISCOURSE

David G. Hunter
University of St. Thomas

ABSTRACT

This paper argues that a key issue in Clement of Alexandria's debate with Gnostic and Encratite Christians was the proper use of language to describe sexual desire and sexual restraint. Against the heretical tendency (evident in both libertine and ascetical writers) to regard "desire" under a single aspect (*epithumia*), Clement deliberately expanded the discourse and used several different terms to describe different facets of "desire" (*epithumia, orexis, hormē*). By so doing, Clement was able to acknowledge the dangers of desire as well as the proper use of desire. Similarly, his discussion of the restraint of desire by virtue (*enkrateia, sōphrosynē*) was fuller and more differentiated than that of his opponents. Clement was thus able to offer an alternative ascetical discourse that was at once more comprehensive and more humane.

Clement of Alexandria has left to posterity one of the most extensive discussions of sexuality and marriage to be found in the patristic age. Not until Augustine's *De bono coniugali* does there appear a work which focuses such sustained attention on the value of Christian marriage and the attendant problem of sexual desire. Michel Foucault has reminded us that the history of sexuality can be written as the history of a discourse about sexuality (1978). This essay is intended as a modest contribution to such a history.[1]

My central argument is that Clement's debate with Gnostic, Marcionite, and especially Encratite forms of Christian asceticism was as much a debate about language as about practice. Specifically, it was a debate about the language appropriate to an ethical description of sexual desire and of sexual restraint. Clement's refutation of Gnostic and Encratite views involved both the vindication of a Christian discourse on desire and a reappropriation of a classical discourse on virtue. While still broadly "ascetic" (i.e. emphasizing restraint), Clement's approach to marriage and sexuality was far more moderate than that of his opponents.

I will proceed in three steps. First, I will discuss the various positions which Clement attempted to refute. Both the libertine and the ascetical perspectives of Clement's opponents, I will suggest, offered a restricted and monochrome view of sexual desire, one that causes him to respond with a broader and more differentiated account of desire. Second, turning to Clement, I will examine the highly variegated language that he employs when discussing sexual desire. No less than three terms appear (*epithumia, orexis, hormē*), each describing a different facet of sexual desire. Only by attending carefully to Clement's highly differentiated vocabulary, I will argue, can we determine the precise contours of his views on sexual desire.[2]

Finally, I will turn to Clement's discussion of the restraint of desire by virtue. Here, too, his language is carefully chosen and dependent on the prior distinctions he makes regarding desire. The terms *enkrateia* and *sōphrosynē* are the key ones here. Both terms have a special role to play in Clement's defense of marriage; both are also related to the varied states of desire I will discuss. We will see Clement consciously and explicitly trying to expand the meaning of the term *enkrateia* beyond the narrow confines of ascetic discourse. In short, my purpose here is to show how great a part of Clement's response to the "heretics" was in fact a discourse about discourse.[3]

Part One: The Language of the "Heretics"

The focus of this essay is the third *Stromata*, which presents Clement's most developed thoughts on marriage, as well as his most explicit attack on the proponents of sexual renunciation.[4] Clement begins with a survey of the various opinions of Gnostic thinkers; Valentinus, Basilides, and Marcion all fall under his scrutiny.[5] He also discusses Plato and the Pythagoreans, whose views on the soul and its imprisonment in the body as a chastisement are, as Clement sees it, the ultimate source of some of the Gnostic errors.[6] But before delving into the issue of sexual renunciation, Clement first takes on the views of the so-called "libertine" Christians. His discussion requires further attention.

Clement devotes a significant portion of the *Stromata* to the views of Carpocrates, Epiphanes, and the followers of Nicolaus, who allegedly advocated free sex.[7] Citing fragments from a treatise by Epiphanes called "Concerning Righteousness," Clement suggests that a discouse on desire lay at the root of this anti-ascetic system. "God made all things for man to be common property," Epiphanes wrote. "He brought female to be with male and in the same way united all animals.... With a view to the permanence of the human race, he has implanted in males a strong and ardent desire (*epithumian*) which neither law nor custom nor any other restraint is able to destoy. For it is God's decree."[8] According to the fragments quoted by Clement, Epiphanes based his practice of free love on the intractable fact of human sexual desire (*epithumia*). The very indiscriminate and unrestrained character of sexual desire, in the libertine view, is warrant for an unrestricted use of sexual relations.

Clement's response is to address directly this question of desire. He first lists the various biblical texts where "desire," specifically designated as *epithumia*, is explicitly forbidden.[9] Later in the third *Stromata*, when summing up his objections to the libertines, Clement addresses the problem of "desire" even more directly. The choice between self-control and the lack of it, between *enkrateia* and *akrasia*, Clement argues, is not a matter of indifference.[10] While claiming to be free from restraint, the libertine is actually enslaved to the body. The person who is "self-controlled," by contrast (Clement's word is *sōphrōn*), "liberates from its passions his soul which is master of the body."[11]

The shape of Clement's argument is a familiar one. He borrows from popular moral philosophy (of both Stoic and Platonic varieties), which often portrayed vice in terms of enslavement to passion. Against the libertine view Clement emphasizes the suppression of *epithumia* and appeals to the notions of *enkrateia* and *sōphrosynē*. What is significant here is that a single term takes a predominant role in Clement's refutation of the libertines: *epithumia*. It is *epithumia* on which Epiphanes based his discourse of indulgence; it is *epithumia*, therefore, which Clement rejects as unbecoming the Christian.[12] As Clement puts it: "We must not live as if there were no difference between right and wrong, but, to the best of our power, must purify ourselves from indulgence (*tōn hēdonōn*) and lust (*tōn epithumiōn*) and take care for our soul which must continually be devoted to the Deity alone."[13] In Clement's own lexicon of desire, therefore, the term *epithumia* became irrevocably associated with the unrestrained use of sex advocated by the libertines, and *enkrateia* was proposed as the orthodox Christian alternative.

Although Clement has presented a fairly extensive discussion of the libertine view, one suspects that this was not the most pressing issue. The bulk of the third *Stromata* is devoted to a discussion of those Christians who advocated the view precisely opposite to that of Carpocrates and Epiphanes, that is, compulsory sexual renunciation. In this second half of his work Clement is no longer dealing with Gnostics of either the ascetic or libertine variety. He has turned his attention to several writers who can generically be labeled as "Encratite."[14] Clement mentions two of them by name: Tatian and Julius Cassian. Furthermore, there is good reason for regarding the latter as the primary target of Clement's polemic.

Throughout this second portion of the third *Stromata* Clement refers repeatedly to the *Gospel According to the Egyptians*, an apocryphal text probably composed in Egypt during the first half of the second century (Hennecke-Schneemelcher: 177–78). The first few times he mentions the text Clement simply notes that his opponents are fond of citing the *Gospel According to the Egyptians*, but he does not indicate who the opponents are. Towards the end of his work, however, Clement clearly identifies Julius Cassian as the writer who makes such great use of the apocryphal text. It will be useful to clarify what we can of Julius' views and how he interpreted the *Gospel According to the Egyptians* in order to understand precisely the nature of Clement's response.

As Clement tells us, Julius was the author of a book, *Peri enkrateias ē peri eunouchias*, that is, "Concerning *Enkrateia* or Celibacy." Although Julius is widely regarded as a major figure in the Encratite movement of the late second century, very little is actually known about him.[15] Clement is virtually our only source on Julius. From the title of his work it is clear that *enkrateia*, understood as absolute sexual renunciation, was his primary concern. Clement tells us that Julius cited with approval Jesus' blessing on those who have become eunuchs for the sake of the kingdom of heaven.[16] According to Clement, Julius also followed the teaching of Tatian, who regarded the devil and not God as the creator of the sexual organs and the author of marriage.[17]

Later Clement makes Julius' views even more precise: "This worthy fellow thinks in Platonic fashion that the soul is of divine origin and, having become female by desire (*epithumia*), has come down here from above to birth and corruption."[18] As Clement portrays him, Julius Cassian adhered to the view, currently popular among Middle Platonists, that the human soul, originally neither male nor female, fell into the material world as a result of an original sin. This primal sin, characterized by Julius as "desire" (*epithumia*), is the cause of human birth. All human sexuality and procreation, in Julius' view, are merely participation in sin and corruption. The aim of salvation as brought by Christ is to recapture the primal innocence of the pre-lapsarian state by repudiating marriage and procreation, thus eliminating all "male and female."[19]

It was in the light of these views that Julius Cassian interpreted the *Gospel According to the Egyptians*. To take one example, Clement tells us that his opponents like to disparage God's creation "under the fair name of *enkrateia*." They quote the Savior's saying in the *Gospel According to the Egyptians*: "I came to destroy the works of the female." The Encratite interpretation, Clement tells us, is that "female" refers to "desire" (*epithumia*) and "works" refers to birth and corruption. In other words, *epithumia*, the cause of the soul's descent into the material world, is also the sexual desire which perpetuates the imprisonment of the soul in the body through procreation.

Clement's answer to the Encratite, significantly, does not dispute the veracity of the dominical saying. Jesus did come "to abolish the works of the female," as Clement sees it, and "female" does refer to "desire." What Clement does, however, is to reform the meaning of the term "desire." *Epithumia*, in his view, does not refer to sexual desire *per se*. The works of *epithumia* which the Lord came to destroy are "the love of money, contentiousness, vanity, mad lust for women, paederasty, gluttony, licentiousness, and similar vices."[20] In other words, Clement redefines the term *epithumia* and removes it from the exclusively sexual context in which it functioned for the Encratite. He expands its connotations to include a whole array of different and non-sexual "desires."[21]

In short, both of Clement's main opponents in the third *Stromata* have based their different views on similarly restrictive notions of "desire." Both the libertine Epiphanes and the Encratite Julius Cassian, as cited by Clement, have developed diverse attitudes towards human sexuality using a similar notion of *epithumia*. For the libertine *epithumia* was the overwhelming urge towards sexual relations which operated indiscriminately of marriage and which contravened any order, custom, or law. *Epithumia* in the libertine view was then exalted into an absolute moral imperative; it was, as Epiphanes noted, "God's decree." The Encratite Julius Cassian likewise made "desire" or *epithumia* a touchstone of his system; like Epiphanes, he made it synonymous with sexual desire. The only difference (and it is a significant one) is that in the Encratite view "desire" (*epithumia*) is both cause and symptom of the first sin. As such, *epithumia* was something to be repudiated and, indeed, it was the primary object of the Encratite *enkrateia*.

Part Two: The Language of Desire

The foregoing discussion has shown, I believe, how central the term *epithumia* was to the second-century heretical discourse on marriage and sexuality. It is now time to turn to Clement and to examine his own discussion of desire. My central argument here is that Clement responds to both the libertine and the Encratite discussions by developing a highly differentiated and nuanced account of desire. Borrowing from a variety of philosophical sources, Clement introduces several terms to characterize human sexual desire. By doing so, he makes possible a retrieval of the goodness of desire, while granting to his ascetic opponents their own sense of the dangers of desire.

The terms *epithumia*, *orexis*, and *hormē*, occur regularly in Clement's discussions of marriage. In one place *epithumia* is said to have a special relationship to marriage. As Clement puts it, "marriage seems to fall under [the rubric of] pleasure and *epithumia*."[22] Similarly, the term *orexis* is central to Clement's discussion of marriage. In one place he defines marriage as "the *orexis* for procreation."[23] Although both of these terms are often translated into English as "desire," there is a very important difference between them. The former is nearly always used in a negative sense, the latter nearly always in a positive sense. It is critical to note the distinction between the two in order to understand which sort of desire Clement approves and which he disapproves.

Epithumia is the term that appears most frequently in Clement's discussions of the dangers of desire. Usually it has the connotation of an excessive or inappropriate desire, what could properly be called "lust." This is the sense that the term usually had in the New Testament and in most of early Christian literature before Clement (Bauer: 293).[24] This was also, as we have seen, the primary sense of the term as used by Clement's libertine and Encratite opponents. Although Clement's usage was influenced by both of these sources, there is another factor at work as well, the ethical theory of Middle Platonism.

It was the merit of Salvatore Lilla's fine book on Clement to have drawn attention to the great impact of Middle Platonism, Neoplatonism and the philosophy of Philo on Clement's ethical thought (60–117). Lilla demonstrated convincingly that Clement made use of the tripartite division of the soul, as first articulated in Plato's *Republic* (4.436a): the *logistikon*, the *thumoeides*, and the *epithumētikon*, what we might call the "rational," the "emotional," and the "desiring" or "concupiscible" parts of the soul (79–84). Each was located respectively in a different part of the body, i.e. the head, the heart, and the liver.[25] Proceeding from the "concupiscible" part of the soul, *epithumia* by definition represents an "irrational" impulse, one which exists prior to the imposition of reason and which, moreover, tends by its very nature to run contrary to reason.[26] *Epithumia*, therefore, in the Middle Platonic view cannot be anything but an irrational "desire" to be resisted by virtue.

But this Middle Platonic teaching on the tripartite soul did more than simply contribute to Clement's decidedly negative use of the term *epithumia*; it also pointed the way towards a solution of the Encratite problem. Clement explicitly refers to the tripartite division of the soul at several places in the third *Stromata*, all of them dealing with the Encratites. In one place, he is discussing the text of Matt 18:20: Where two or three are gathered in the name of Christ, there is the Lord. Among the several exegetical options, Clement suggests that the "three" may be *thumos, epithumia,* and *logismos*, that is, the Middle Platonic triad of feeling, desire, and reason.[27] Clement goes on to say that there is a proper use of the soul's natural powers and even an appropriate "desire" (he uses the verb *epithumei*), as long as reason (*logismos*) holds sway. Ultimately, however, the true Gnostic will rise above *thumos* and *epithumia* and begin to love the creation and God its Creator. Then there will be true *enkrateia*, which derives from a union of knowledge, faith, and love.

We will return to this notion of the true *enkrateia* in the final portion of this paper. Here I wish to show how this tripartite division of the soul helped Clement to deal with the Encratite challenge, specifically the views of Julius Cassian. Julius, as I have noted, frequently appealed to the *Gospel According to the Egyptians*. Julius had cited the following verses from the work, as quoted by Clement:

> When Salome asked when she would know the answer to her questions, the Lord said, When you trample on the robe of shame, and when the two shall be one, and the male with the female, and there is neither male nor female.[28]

Julius, of course, had interpreted this as a command to repudiate the body and, specifically, sexual relations.

Clement's response, again, is not to dispute the authenticity of the saying (although he does note that it is not found in any of the canonical gospels). Rather, he says that Julius has failed to understand that the "male" impulse refers to *thumos* and the "female" to *epithumia*. "When these operate," Clement writes, "they lead to repentance and shame." Clement then proposes that the true interpretation of the saying is that people must not be led by *thumos* and *epithumia*, but rather by *logismos*. In other words, the lower powers of the soul must be submitted to the higher one of reason, thereby allowing for a proper unity of the person in obedience to the Logos, what Clement describes as a unity of spirit (*pneuma*) and soul (*psychē*).

What we have here, in essence, is Clement's response to the Encratite problem of *epithumia*. A proper understanding of the human person, Clement argues, will take into account that *epithumia* (and *thumos* as well) are powers of the soul that need to be regulated by reason (Völker: 130–32). In other words, it is possible for there to be a proper ordering of these lower desires, and not simply their suppression. This is where the other two terms for "desire" become relevant, for Clement will proceed to discuss the problem of human sexuality by employing other terms for these rationally ordered desires. *Orexis* and *hormē* are both terms used in Clement's alternative discourse on desire and both terms help him to develop dimensions of desire well beyond those of his opponents. While *epithumia* nearly always means "an evil desire," the other terms for desire (*orexis* and *hormē*) nearly always connote the opposite.

Clement himself is quite explicit on this point. In a passage from the fourth *Stromata*, which concerns the centrality of love (*agapē*) in the life of the Christian Gnostic, Clement discusses the difference between *epithumia* and proper love. *Epithumia* or "lust" seizes on appearances or physical beauty; chaste love (*agapē hagnē*), on the other hand, looks upon the beauty of the body as it would a beautiful statue and sees beyond the work of art to the Artisan and true beauty that is spiritual.[29] Then, in a pair of sentences critical to the argument of this paper, Clement writes: "Those who are skilled in these matters make a distinction between *orexis* and *epithumia*. They assign *epithumia* to the pleasures and licentiousness, since it is irrational; but they assign *orexis* to the necessities of nature, since it consists in a rational movement."[30]

As this text indicates, Clement is quite capable of conceiving desire in both positive and negative terms: there were rational and irrational desires. Proper desire, that is a well-ordered natural desire, was usually designated as an *orexis*; a negative or irrational desire, what we might call "lust," was designated as *epithumia*. The point is not merely a pedantic one. Numerous scholars have suggested that Clement is rather hostile to the fact of human sexual desire. John Ferguson, for example, suggests that "Clement's ideal is not to feel sexual desire, and to let sexual union be determined wholly by will" (131). John Oulton and Henry Chadwick, in their introduction to the only English translation of the third *Stromata*, suggest that Clement's ideal Christian "is not to feel anything at all" (34).

If my analysis is correct, such comments are based on a failure to acknowledge the various terms that Clement uses for "desire." Many texts can be cited to support the position that Clement advocated a repudiation of "desire," but in each case the sort of desire being rejected is *epithumia*.[31] Attention to the other terms which may be rendered as "desire" will show that Clement was also capable of articulating a positive understanding of human desire, and of human sexual desire in particular.

To take *orexis* again. Unlike *epithumia* and *thumos*, the term *orexis* does not occur in Plato. It apparently was coined by Aristotle, and later adopted by the Stoics, in order to express the active, rather than passive, experience of "desire" (Nussbaum: 273–74). The term *orexis*, at least in Aristotle, emphasized the animal's directedness towards an object that subsumes and in some sense unifies the three parts of the Platonic soul (275). Clement seems to be aware of this Stoic and Aristotelian use of the term *orexis*, for he often uses the term *orexis* in conjunction with some modifier such as "natural" or "in accordance with nature" (Clark: 43,48,56).

For example, I have already mentioned the brief definition of marriage as an *orexis* or "desire for procreation." And, as we have seen, Clement could clearly distinguish an irrational *epithumia* from a natural and rational *orexis*. In Clement *orexis* could designate the natural desires or appetites of the human person, including sexual desires. In one place, for example, while commenting on 1 Cor 7:5, Clement refers to the persistence of sexual desires (without any hint of disapproval) in terms of the "urges of nature" (*tēs physeōs orexeis*).[32] Elsewhere he speaks of "desires" (*orexeis*) that are "according to nature," by which he means fully acceptable to the Christian.[33] Only when carried to excess or when turned against nature do the *orexeis* lead to sin. In this case the natural or rational desire becomes, according to the classic Stoic definition, an *epithumia* or an *orexis alogos* (Inwood: 228).[34]

One reason it seems that Clement could regard *orexis* as a rational form of desire was that *orexis* was not in itself strictly physical. This point is confirmed by a brief, but suggestive comment in the third *Stromata*. Here Clement is responding to the view of a particular heretic who suggested that the top half of the human body is the work of a divine craftsman, but that the bottom half is the work of inferior creators and therefore liable to the desire for intercourse (*oregesthai sunousias*). He finds fault with the heretical view on several scores. First, it errs by locating desire only in the lower part of the body; the upper portion of a human being, Clement argues, is also subject to "desire," such as the desire for food. Furthermore, Clement writes, "desire (*orexis*) is not a bodily thing, although it originates through [or "because of"] the body."[35] In other words, *orexis* itself, while it takes the form of bodily desire, is not a mere physical impulse; it is rather that physical impulse rationally ordered to the proper use of nature.

This takes me to the third term in Clement's lexicon of desire, the word *hormē*. *Hormē* and *orexis* are rather close in meaning, although there is a significant difference between them. *Hormē* was the Stoic term for "a natural impulse" and it was a commonly accepted criterion for the presence of an animal soul (Inwood: 255). *Hormē*, therefore, in the Stoic view represents the more strictly biological side of natural desire, whereas *orexis* tends to be used in a more abstract sense for a desire confirmed by rational choice. Like *orexis*, however, *hormē* refers to a power of the soul, one that inclines the person in one direction or another.

Take, for example, this definition of passion (*pathos*) which is found in Clement's second *Stromata*:[36]

> *Hormē* is the movement of the mind to or from something. Passion is an excessive *hormē*, one that exceeds the measures of reason, or a *hormē* that is unbridled and disobedient to reason. Passions, then, are a perturbation of the soul contrary to nature, in disobedience to reason. . . . If one examines each of the passions he will find them to be irrational desires (*alogous orexeis*).

In this text *hormē* is used in what appears to be a fairly neutral sense. As a movement of the mind, it can impel the person in either a good and rational direction or in a bad and irrational direction. This is confirmed by other passages in Clement where *hormē* is described as the soul's power or capability to be moved in one direction or another. As Clement noted in the first *Stromata*, the soul must have the power of *hormē* and *aphormē*, that is, the power of inclination or disinclination, in order for there to be genuine freedom.[37]

If my analysis of Clement's language is correct, we have three terms which describe human desire, and human sexual desire in particular, under three different aspects. If *epithumia* refers to "desire" in its irrational and unrestrained dimension, and if *orexis* refers primarily to the rationally ordered expression of desire, *hormē* functions as a kind of neutral, middle ground between the two. It refers to the basic fact of human desire or capacity for movement which can be turned either towards a natural and rational desire (*orexis*) or towards an excessive, disordered and irrational use (*epithumia*).[38]

There is at least one text in Clement that illustrates the interaction of these three terms perfectly. In the third *Stromata*, after introducing the problematic of the Encratites, Clement turns to the scriptures and proceeds to discuss "all of the biblical texts which oppose these heretical sophists and show the right rule of self-control (*enkrateia*) that is preserved in accordance with reason."[39] He cites several passages, including "Thou shalt not covet thy neighbor's wife" (Ex 20:17) and the saying of Jesus, "Do not lust" (Mt 5:27).

Then, in an attempt to define the sort of self-restraint that characterizes Christian *enkrateia*, Clement refers to a prescription in the Hebrew Scriptures that forbids unmarried men from having immediate sexual relations with captive women.[40] "If the man has conceived a desire for her (*epithumēsantos*)," Clement writes, "he is directed to mourn for thirty days while she is to have her hair cut; if after this the desire (*epithumia*) has not passed off, then they may proceed to beget children, because the appointed time enables the dominating impulse (*hormē*) to be tested and to become a rational desire" (*orexis eulogos*).[41]

In this passage Clement links each of the three terms for "desire" that I have been discussing. The mediating term appears to be *hormē*. The impulse to have sexual relations, which is itself morally neutral, can be turned either towards a good or a bad use. Left unchecked or unrestrained, it stands in danger of becoming an *epithumia*. But properly tested by time and directed towards the begetting of children, the natural impulse (*hormē*) is capable of becoming a rational desire (*orexis*).[42] The function of the virtue of *enkrateia* is precisely to channel the neutral "impulse" (*hormē*) towards the proper use of nature.

What, then, is the ultimate point of Clement's highly nuanced and complex analysis of desire? Under the influence of Middle Platonic philosophy and in harmony with much of earlier Christian tradition,

Clement was deeply aware of the dangers of desire; that is, he was concerned about the tendency for physical pleasure to become an end in itself. This accounts for the way in which he constantly links *epithumia* with *hēdonē*, in line with much of traditional Greco-Roman philosophy. On the other hand, the same philosophical tradition provided Clement with the terminology to speak of a neutral experience of sexual desire (*hormē*), as well as its more conscious and rational counterpart, the *orexis eulogos*.

Furthermore, all three terms proved useful to Clement in his debate with the libertine Gnostics and Encratites. Clement's negative use of *epithumia* allowed him to emphasize the suppression of this tendency, especially against the libertine exaltation of *epithumia*. This also helped him to meet some of the ascetic concerns of the Encratites. On the other hand, Clement's use of the terms *orexis* and *hormē* enabled him to broaden his discourse on desire, making room for a proper and well-ordered experience of desire. Once the possibility of a rational and natural sexual desire is granted, then the door is open for an account of sexual relations within a discourse on virtue.

Part Three: The Language of Virtue

This brings me to the final part of this essay, Clement's terminology for virtue. My final argument is that Clement's discussion of marital virtue betrays a similar linguistic concern as his discussion of desire. Faced with Encratite opponents, who exalted the virtue of complete sexual renunciation (designated as *enkrateia*), Clement gladly embraces the term, but dramatically alters its meaning. On the one hand, he attempts to downplay the sexual aspect of *enkrateia*, arguing that the virtue can be applied to all forms of excessive desire, not merely sexual ones. On the other hand, Clement transforms even the sexual content of the term by using it to characterize the proper and disciplined use of sexual relations in marriage. Both points need to be examined, for in both cases Clement has linked his discussion of virtue to the analysis of desire that I have described thus far in this essay.

On the first point, at several places in the third *Stromata* Clement mentions that *enkrateia* does not pertain solely to the repression of *epithumia* in the sense of sexual desire. "One ought to consider *enkrateia*," he writes, "not merely in relation to one form of it, that is, sexual relations (*ta aphrodisia*), but in relation to all the other indulgences for which the soul craves (*epithumei*) when it is ill content with what is necessary and seeks for luxury. It is *enkrateia* to despise money, softness, property, to hold in small esteem outward appearance, to control one's tongue, to master evil thoughts."[43]

Clement's target in this description of *enkrateia* is clearly the Encratite penchant for exalting one form of restraint: the sexual one. The Encratite, it will be recalled, saw *epithumia* as sexual desire and regarded it as a primary result of the fall. Clement wants to shift the problem of desire to a broader plane. *Enkrateia* is still focused on rooting out and restraining disordered desire or *epithumia*, as the Encratites had claimed. But by emphasizing the different types of disordered desires, Clement is able to diffuse some of the power of the Encratite position. The Encratite *enkrateia*, in Clement's view, is inadequate precisely because it does not cover comprehensively the full range of *epithumiai*. In other words, the virtue of the Encratites does not go far enough because it fails to take account of the many different types of wicked desires.[44]

Of even greater interest is Clement's second linguistic maneuver. For the Encratite *enkrateia* had referred exclusively to celibacy; no other form of renunciation would do (Chadwick: 352-53). Clement, by contrast, deliberately rejects this restrictive use of the term. For him *enkrateia* is linked intimately with *sōphrosynē*, and both terms are freely used to describe the "chaste" or "restrained" use of sex in marriage. Here, again, Clement had the philosophical tradition on his side, for, in contrast to the Encratite usage, the terms *enkrateia* and *sōphrosynē* had been virtually synonymous for much of their history (North: 123-32; Foucault, 1986: 63-77).[45] While it is beyond the scope of this essay to present any comprehensive survey of this history, I can at least point to the manner in which Clement links the two terms and suggest what this may have to do with his varied discourse on desire.

Both *enkrateia* and *sōphrosynē* are frequently described as virtues which are aligned against the vices or passions, particularly against *epithumia* and *hēdonē*.[46] As such, both terms have a special function to perform in sexual matters, although, as we have seen, Clement took care not to limit *enkrateia* to the sexual domain. Often the two terms are indistinguishable in Clement. Where they are distinguished, the main difference seems to be that *sōphrosynē* lacks the combative dimension that characterizes *enkrateia*. As Jean-Paul Broudéhoux has put it: "These two virtues control sexual activity under different aspects: whereas temperance [*sōphrosynē*] is concerned with regulating in a positive manner the use of the intimate relations in marriage, continence [*enkrateia*] intervenes especially to prevent any sexual abuse and to 'desensualize' the marriage, that is, to relieve it of any attachment to the passions" (122-23).

For the purposes of this study the significance of Clement's discussion of these virtues is the way in which the terms are used to structure an argument against the Encratites. Against the heretical ascetics who reject marriage and demand their own brand of *enkrateia*, that is, absolute sexual renunciation, Clement proposes a rival, more moderate ideal of *enkrateia*. Through the virtues of *enkrateia* and *sōphrosynē*, he writes, not only the spirit, but also our behavior, our way of life, and even our bodies are being sanctified.[47] In a manner that anticipates some of Augustine's teaching on marriage and celibacy, Clement insists that authentic *enkrateia* is interior: "it is a virtue of the soul which is not manifest to others, but is in secret."[48] Most importantly, *enkrateia* was to proceed from a love of God, not from a contempt for creation: "We set high value on self-control when it arises from love to the Lord and seeks that which is good for its own sake, sanctifying the temple of the Holy Spirit."[49]

The virtues of *enkrateia* and *sōphrosynē*, therefore, have a very intimate relation with the varied states of desire I have described. *Enkrateia* is especially concerned with rooting out the hedonistic, self-centered lust characterized by the term *epithumia*. *Sōphrosynē*, for its part, is most concerned with the elevation of the natural, created "impulses" (*hormai*) and their transformation into rational, well-ordered desires (*orexeis*). That is why Clement will often modify the word "marriage" (*gamos*) with the adjective *sōphrōn*, or link it with *sōphrosynē*.[50] That is why, too, he can refer to sexual relations for the sake of procreation as a "chaste" (*enkratōs*) use of marriage, wherein all lust (*epithumia*) is extinguished.[51]

In short, Clement's discourse on desire has carried him into a discourse on virtue, wherein the narrow content of the Encratite *enkrateia* has been dramatically reshaped. The monolithic and monochrome Encratite picture of desire as sexual and sinful has given way to a discourse that recognizes the possibility of various and good desires. And the restrictive Encratite notion of *enkrateia* as sexual renunciation has yielded to a broader vision, wherein the virtue of "self-restraint" applies to "desires" other than sexual ones, as well as to the proper expression even of sexual desire. The result is a more humane vision of the person and a more tolerant discourse on virtue.

NOTES

[1] Clement's thought on marriage has been given a thorough treatment by Jean-Paul Broudéhoux (1972), who provides a full bibliography. See also Mees (1977)

[2] A perusal of the standard English translations of Clement's works will reveal that the proper distinctions between the different terms for "desire" have not always been made. Translators have tended to homogenize the various Greek words.

[3] It is true that Clement's language is not always precise, and that due allowance must be made for some slippage between meanings; cf. the comments of Broudéhoux (12). Nevertheless, the distinctions offered in this essay will be substantiated both by their repeated occurrence in Clement's work and by their appearance in other writers.

[4] Clement's work will be cited according to the critical edition of Otto Stählin (1905, 1906, 1909).

[5] *Str.* III.1.1–2 (Valentinus and Basilides); III.3.12 and 4.25 (Marcion).

6 *Str.* III.3.13–24.
7 *Str.* III.2.5–11 (Carpocrates and Epiphanes); III.4.26–49 (Nicolaus and others).
8 *Str.* III.2.8 (Stählin: 199); trans. Oulton and Chadwick: 43–44.
9 For example, Matt 5:28 and Exod 20:17, cited in *Str.* III.2.8.
10 *Str.* III.5.41.
11 *Ibid.* (Stählin: 214); trans. Oulton and Chadwick: 58.
12 Cf. *Str.* III.5.41 (Stählin: 214): "For desire (*epithumia*) is nourished and invigorated if it is encouraged in indulgence, just as, on the other hand, it loses strength if it is kept in check." Trans. Oulton and Chadwick: 59.
13 *Str.* III.5.42 (Stählin: 215); trans. Oulton and Chadwick: 59.
14 Clement does not use this term in the third *Stromata*. He does, however, use it in several other places: *Str.* I.71.5 and VII.108.2, and *Paedagogus* II.32.4; cited in Broudéhoux (42).
15 Julius is often mentioned as a typical Encratite thinker in the recent volume of essays edited by U. Bianchi (1985). Strangely, however, the volume contains no extensive discussion of his views.
16 *Str.* III.13.91; cf. III.6.50, where Matt 19:11f. is explicitly cited.
17 *Str.* III.12.80–81.
18 *Str.* III.13.93 (Stählin: 239); trans. Oulton and Chadwick: 84, slightly altered.
19 The link between this Encratite view of original sin and all later accounts, especially Augustine's, has been argued by P.F. Beatrice (1978).
20 *Str.* III.9.63 (Stählin: 225); trans. Oulton and Chadwick: 69.
21 A similar point is made when Clement responds to Julius' use of the *Gospel of the Egyptians*. Julius had cited the following passage to support his call to celibacy: "When Salome asked when she would know the answer to her questions, the Lord said, When you trample on the robe of shame, and when the two shall be one, and the male with the female, and there is neither male nor female." Clement responds that Julius fails to understand what is meant by "male" and "female." The male impulse refer to *thumos*, Clement suggests, and the female to *epithumia*. See our discussion of these terms below.
22 *Str.* II.23.137 (Stählin: 188).
23 *Paed.* II.10.95 (Stählin, 1905: 214).
24 Clement frequently cites a number of biblical texts forbidding *epithumia*, thereby demonstrating the influence of these texts upon him. See *Str.* III.11.71 and III.14.94 (Matt 5:27); *Str.* III.11.76 (Rom 7:7); *Str.* III.7.58 (Rom 13:14).
25 Furthermore, Lilla (86–92) showed that Clement also made use of the Middle Platonic notion (found also in Possidonius, Plutarch, Philo, and others) that the origins of the passions (*pathē*) lay in the irrational part of the soul most closely associated with the body, namely the *epithumētikon*.
26 Lilla (92) cites a passage from Philo (*Leg. Alleg.* 3.115), which defines *epithumia* as an *orexis alogos*.
27 *Str.* III.10.68.
28 *Str.* III.13.92 (Stählin: 238); trans. Oulton and Chadwick: 83.
29 *Str.* IV.18.116 (Stählin: 299).
30 *Str.* IV.18.117 (Stählin: 300).
31 For example, in *Str.* III.5.42 Clement refers to the need to be "purified from *hēdonē* and *epithumia*" in order to be formed in God's image. In *Str.* III.7.57 Clement remarks that whereas the pagan philosopher struggles against "desire," the Christian ideal "is not to experience desire (*epithumia*) at all." Cf. III.7.58.
32 *Str.* III.12.82 (Stählin: 233). Clement is responding to Tatian's use of 1 Cor 7 to forbid sexual intercourse.
33 *Str.* II.20.109 (Stählin: 172).
34 Only very rarely is *orexis* used by Clement to designate an evil desire. An example occurs in *Str.* III.96, where *orexis* is qualified as "a desire for alien pleasures."

35 *Str.* III.4.34 (Stählin: 211). This passage from Clement echoes a sentiment of Plato, *Philebus* 35C. In the text Socrates goes on to argue that "it is to the soul that all impulse and desire, and indeed the determining principle of the whole creature, belong."
36 *Str.* II.13.59 (Stählin: 145). Lilla (84–86) has noted that this definition is based on Stoic terminology and goes back to Zeno and Chrysippus.
37 *Str.* I.17.83–84 (Stählin: 54); cf. VI.8.68–69 (Stählin: 468).
38 A clear parallel to this use of *orexis* and *epithumia* is found in Plutarch's *Amatorius* 750c-e. See the very helpful commentary by Foucault (1986: 199–200).
39 *Str* III.11.71 (Stählin: 228).
40 Deut 21:11–13. The same biblical passage is also cited in *Str.* II.18.88–89.
41 *Str.* III.11.71 (Stählin: 228).
42 Clement's interpretation of this story is borrowed from Philo. See his *De virtutibus* 110–115, and the discussion in Annawies van den Hoek (88–90). Van den Hoek (90) notes that Clement alters both the order and the wording of Philo's text: "By his exclusions, Clement tends to emphasize control of the passions. A union is not based both on love and procreation, as in Philo, but exclusively on the latter."
43 *Str.* III.7.59 (Stählin: 223); tran. Oulton and Chadwick: 67, slightly altered. Similar sentiments are found in *Str.* III.1.4.
44 Here again the philosophical tradition was of some help to Clement, for there was in Aristotle a discussion of *enkrateia* precisely in this broader context. See *Nicomachean Ethics* VII.4; cited in Elizabeth A. Clark (55).
45 For the relation of the two terms in Clement, see Broudéhoux (120–124, 127–131, and the important note on 21–22). On *enkrateia* alone, see Chadwick (1960).
46 See *Str.* II.18.79; III.6.54; IV.23.151; also Broudéhoux (122) and Lilla (78ff.).
47 *Str.* III.6.47.
48 *Str.* III.6.48.
49 *Str.* III.7.59.
50 Among many references, see *Str.* III.9.67, III.12.81 and III.12.86.
51 *Str.* III.15.96.

WORKS CONSULTED

Bauer, Walter
    1979   *A Greek-English Lexicon of the New Testament and Other Early Christian Literature.* Tr. William F. Arndt and F. Wilbur Gingrich. Rev. and aug. F.W. Gingrich and Frederick W. Danker. Chicago: University of Chicago Press.

Beatrice, Pier F.
    1978   *Tradux peccati. Alle fonti della dottrina agostiniana del peccato originale.* Milan: Vita e Pensiero.

Bianchi, Ugo
    1985   *La tradizione dell'Enkrateia. Motivazione ontologiche et protologiche.* Rome: Edizioni dell'Ateneo.

Broudéhoux, Jean-Paul
    1972   *Mariage et famille chez Clément d'Alexandrie.* Théologie Historique 11. Paris: Beauchesne.

Chadwick, Henry
    1960   "Enkrateia." *RAC* 5:343–365.

Clark, Elizabeth A.
    1977   *Clement's Use of Aristotle: The Aristotelian Contribution to Clement of Alexandria's Refutation of Gnosticism*. Texts and Studies in Religion. New York: Edwin Mellen.

Ferguson, John
    1974   *Clement of Alexandria*. New York: Twayne.

Foucault, Michel
    1978   *The History of Sexuality*. Vol. 1: *An Introduction*. Tr. Robert Hurley. New York: Random House.
    1986   *The History of Sexuality*. Vol. 3: *The Care of the Self*. Tr. Robert Hurley. New York: Random House.

Hennecke, Edgar and Wilhelm Schneemelcher
    1963   *New Testament Apocrypha*. Vol 1: *Gospels and Related Writings*. English translation edited by R. McL. Wilson. Philadelphia: Westminster.

Inwood, Brad
    1985   *Ethics and Human Action in Early Stoicism*. Oxford: Clarendon; New York: Oxford University Press.

Lilla, Salvatore
    1971   *Clement of Alexandria: A Study in Christian Platonism and Gnosticism*. Oxford Theological Monographs. Oxford: Oxford University Press.

Mees, Michael
    1977   "Clemens von Alexandrien über Ehe und Familie." *Augustinianum* 17:113–131.

North, Helen
    1966   *SOPHROSYNE: Self-Knowledge and Self-Restraint in Greek Literature*. Ithaca, NY: Cornell University Press.

Nussbaum, Martha
    1986   *The Fragility of Goodness: Luck and Ethics in Greek Tragedy and Philosophy*. Cambridge: Cambridge University Press.

Oulton, John Ernest Leonard and Henry Chadwick
    1954   *Alexandrian Christianity*. LCC 2. Philadelphia: Westminster.

Prunet, Olivier
 1966 *La morale de Clément d'Alexandrie et le Nouveau Testament.* Études d'Histoire et de Philosophie Religieuses 61. Paris: Presses Universitaires de France.

Stählin, Otto
 1905 *Clemens Alexandrinus.* Erster Band. *Protrepticus und Paedagogus.* GCS 12. Leipzig: J.C. Hinrichs.
 1906 *Clemens Alexandrinus.* Zweiter Band. *Stromata Buch I-VI.* GCS 15. Leipzig: J.C. Hinrichs.
 1909 *Clemens Alexandrinus.* Dritter Band. *Stromata Buch VII und VII—Excerpta ex Theodoto—Eclogae propheticae—Quis dives Salvetur—Fragmente.* GCS 17. Leipzig: J.C. Hinrichs.

Van den Hoek, Annawies
 1988 *Clement of Alexandria and His Use of Philo in the Stromateis: An Early Christian Reshaping of a Jewish Model.* Supplements to Vigiliae Christianae 3. Leiden: Brill.

Völker, Walther
 1952 *Der wahre Gnostiker nach Clemens Alexandrinus.* TU 57. Berlin: Akademie-Verlag; Leipzig: J.C. Hinrichs.

ALLEGORY AND ASCETICISM IN GREGORY OF NYSSA

Verna E. F. Harrison
Berkeley, CA

Gregory of Nyssa, a deeply traditional and highly original fourth–century Christian thinker, uses allegory to enable Scripture to address the needs of an ascetic audience. His exegetical method establishes a bridge from the written word to the contemporary philosophical, theological and social context of the reading community, and to each individual's practical and spiritual situation within it. Moreover, the interpretive move from letter to spiritual meaning directly parallels the ascetic's transfer of attention and desire from material to intelligible realities. Such allegory supports ascetic practice and is supported by it.

Gregory uses this method to interpret texts involving food and erotic love, such as the Manna story in Exodus, Mt 5:6 and the Song of Songs. He sees them as referring to the ascetic's union with God and reception of divine life into the self. In this spirituality, gender is transcended in its literal sense, but in the allegorical sense all human persons function as females, as receptacles impregnated by God, bringing forth virtues or Christ.

In this mode of interpretation, the exegete, like the ascetic, turns away from the Scripture's literal meaning in search of a spiritual meaning beyond it. Yet the material language of the text itself is not bypassed but proves indispensable and functions like the painted colors in an icon, as Gregory himself observes. Meaning is discerned precisely in and through the images of language or color, not apart from them.

Gregory of Nyssa, youngest of the three great Cappadocian fathers of the fourth century, developed a distinctive understanding of the Christian life which articulated his deeply personal spirituality through the thought-forms of a powerful and original philosophical and theological conceptualization. Yet he was also very much a man of his time, familiar with the best contemporary Hellenistic philosophy, science and culture, as well as the varieties of thought and practice current among both highly educated and more simple Christians. He was profoundly influenced by this environment and not least by the ascetical movement in which his sister Macrina and his brother Basil played leading roles. Many of his writings were intended for an audience of ascetics and others who looked to the spirituality and ethical practice of ascetics as an ideal to be imitated as far as their capacities and circumstances allowed.

In late antiquity, allegory served to bring together a sacred text and the concerns of an audience whose *Sitz im Leben* differed from that of the text's original readers (Grant; Bardolle). It established a bridge from the written word to the contemporary philosophical, theological and social context of the community and to each individual's practical and spiritual situation, thus making it immediately relevant to them precisely as Scripture, as a book that could have an impact on their lives (Ford).

For Gregory's primary audience in the ascetic community, where fasting and chastity were highly valued as spiritual practices, biblical texts involving food and sexuality, such as the Manna in the Exodus story and the conjugal love in the Song of Songs, are often pastorally inapplicable in their literal sense. Ascetics can read such materials as Scripture only if they are interpreted in another way. So Gregory finds it appropriate to understand them allegorically.

Moreover, within his broadly Platonic world-view, allegory allows him to transfer the concepts and images of nourishment and intimacy from the material to the intelligible world. In his hands, this deliberate transition from text to interpretation becomes an excellent tool for expressing how the ascetic redirects natural human desire from bodily pleasures toward God. Exegetical method thus comes to mirror ascetic behavior itself and conversely embodies a redirection of thought which can serve as a model for the corresponding redirection of human drives and activities. This paper will consider some of the correspondences between allegory and asceticism in Gregory's writings by looking first at his understanding of allegory and then at some examples of how he uses it in relation to food and erotic love.

In the prologue to his *Commentary on the Song of Songs*, probably in response to criticism from the Antiochene school or elsewhere, he defends and explains his use of allegory (Heine). He rests much of his case on the ways Hebrew Scripture is used in the New Testament and on the Christian community's traditional methods of understanding biblical texts in ways that accord with its theological and ethical teachings.[1] However, he also stresses the purpose of exegesis, which he sees as useful to the reader, and he does not distinguish a meaning he regards as fulfilling this purpose from the original author's intention. He observes that Paul reads Scripture with an eye to what is useful and best for him, and adds that the apostle says it is "written for our instruction" (1 Cor 10:11), i.e. for the benefit of his community as well as himself (Jaeger 6:6). Gregory explains that this usefulness is the criterion for choosing an appropriate mode of interpretation; he assumes the reading which results from such interpretation to be the text's true meaning:

> Thus if the literal sense, as it is called, should be of any use, we will readily have the object of our search. But if anything in the hidden, symbolic sense cannot be of use with regard to the literal sense, we will, as the Word teaches and as Proverbs says (1:6), turn to an understanding of the passage either as a parable, a dark saying, an utterance of wise men, or as a riddle. With regard

to anagogy, it makes no difference what we call it—tropology or allegory—as long as we grasp the meaning of the words (Jaeger 6:4–5; McCambley: 35–36).

Notice that for Gregory the fruits of exegesis are more important than the particular method. If the literal sense is useful, one need not look further, for the goal is achieved, though in practice he and other fathers often do look further, on the assumption that Scripture has multiple levels of meaning. However, if the literal sense proves inappropriate, one has recourse to spiritual exegesis as a tool for discovering something useful. Notice how Gregory lumps all varieties of spiritual exegesis together, since what matters to him is their function, which is always the same (cf. Ford).

For what, then, is the reading of Scripture useful? Gregory explains that both its precepts and its historical narratives teach "knowledge of the mysteries" and "a pure way of life" (Jaeger 6:5; McCambley: 36). Significantly, these two purposes are identical to the two primary goals of Eastern Christian asceticism, namely contemplation, knowledge of the mysteries of God, and action, the acquisition of the virtues. Although this conceptual structure is only fully articulated by Evagrius, the great systematizer of Greek ascetical theology,[2] the issues of action and contemplation are major topics in the ascetical writings of the Cappadocians, who are, after all, Evagrius' teachers. Virtue and communion with God are the central themes in Gregory of Nyssa's *Commentary on the Song of Songs* and many of his other exegetical works. In other words, he uses Scripture to teach the ascetic life, and he acknowledges explicitly that this is his intention. Allegory, with its moral and mystical/theological interpretations, is what enables him to do this.

Moreover, we must remember that for Gregory the virtues are primarily attributes of God and of Christ in which human persons, as bearers of the divine image, can choose to participate. Thus, to acquire virtue is to receive grace, and so the ascetic's life of action through the exercise of virtues already involves the communion with God associated with contemplation (*Or. cat.* 5, Srawley: 19–28; *De prof. Christ.*, Jaeger 8.1:134–35; *De vita Moys.*, Jaeger 7.1:4; Balás; Harrison, 1992: chap. 3). Hence the two sides of asceticism are both ontologically and practically inseparable. The images of food and erotic love, in which the human person plays an active yet receptive role, illustrate this spirituality well, as we shall see.

Gregory emphasizes that the interpreter must have a diligent mind and search the Scriptures in every possible way to find what is true and useful. He asserts that Paul recommends this kind of exegesis and that in the Gospels Christ expects his disciples to receive and ponder his own teachings in the same active way:

> Christ trained his disciples' minds through sayings veiled and hidden in parables, images, obscure words, and terse sayings in riddles. Sometimes he gave an explanation which removed their obscurity. But if the disciples occasionally did not grasp the intent of his words, Christ rebuked their slowness and lack of understanding (Jaeger 6:5–8; McCambley: 37).

Two examples of such rebukes follow, both of which involve food: (1) In Matthew 16:5–12 the disciples misinterpret a warning against the leaven of the Pharisees by relating it to their lack of material bread, and Christ explains that he refers not to physical food but to teaching; (2) In John 4:31–33, as the disciples are concerned about preparing a meal, Christ says, "I have food to eat of which you do not know," and he has to explain further that he means not material food but, in Gregory's words, "the fulfillment of the salvific will" of his Father (Jaeger 6:8–9; McCambley: 37). Thus food ingested by the body comes to represent what is received into the soul, as a disciple accepts teachings into his mind and heart or as the incarnate Son accepts the will of his Father. We will say more later about the place this concept of food holds in Gregory's anthropology.

The training, perseverence and effort Gregory requires of the exegete appear to parallel similar traits in the ascetic. Further analysis of how he characterizes the interpreter's task intensifies and confirms the presence of this parallel. He represents Paul as teaching that "we must pass to an immaterial and intelligible contemplation [of Scripture] so that considerations of the more bodily notion may be changed in the direction of the noetic once the more fleshly appearance of the words has been shaken off like dust" (Jaeger 6:6–7; McCambley: 36). After listing many instances of symbolic and metaphorical language in the Gospels, Gregory again concludes that

> all these and similar examples should serve to remind us of the necessity of searching the divine words, of reading them, and of tracing in every way possible how a more sublime comprehension might be found which leads our mind from the obvious meaning to things more divine and incorporeal (Jaeger 6:9–10; McCambley: 38).

Thus, the exegetical effort involves a deliberate choice to turn away from the literal sense of the text and look for a spiritual meaning. This transfer of attention from sensible to intelligible realities clearly manifests a Platonic world-view, but it also indicates a way of thinking molded by ascetical ideals and discipline. The two examples of food cited above illustrate this. The exegete is asked to bypass the concept of material food in order to find the spiritual nourishment of good teaching and the divine will. This echoes the effort of the ascetic who by fasting empties the body of physical food in the hope that the soul will instead be filled with the presence of Christ, the Bread of life. Both exegete and ascetic use their free choice to redirect desire and attention from matter to spirit.

Gregory goes on to compare Scripture with food more directly. He says that to reject spiritual exegesis is like serving people wheat without removing chaff and husks, grinding the flour and baking it into bread. The uninterpreted word is like food suitable for irrational animals but unfit for consumption by rational human beings (Jaeger 6:12). Lying behind this assertion is the Cappadocian's belief that the difference between beasts and humans is that while both participate in material and biological existence, humans also have rational souls and participate with the angels in the intelligible world (*De opif. hom.* 2 and 18, PG 44:132D-33D, 192A-96B; *Or cat.* 6, Srawley: 28–32). He says in the treatise *On Infants' Early Deaths* that the proper food of intelligible beings is the vision of God and participation in him (Jaeger 3.2:78–80). So when he says that the exegete's task is to make Scripture into human food, his clear implication is that one must find manifestations of intelligible reality in the text. It should serve the reader as a means of communion with God. Good teaching and the divine will also function as food in bringing about such communion.

Let us now turn more specifically to some of Gregory's allegorical interpretations of food, beginning with the Manna of Exodus 16 as explained in the *Life of Moses*. The text says that when the supplies which the Israelites had brought from Egypt ran out, God rained manna on them from heaven which required no preparation and satisfied their desires. Gregory finds the following lesson in this story:

> We learn by what purifications one should purify himself of Egypt and the foreign life so that he empties the bag of his soul of all evil food prepared by the Egyptians. In this way he receives in himself with his pure soul the food which comes down from above (Jaeger 7.1:77; Malherbe and Ferguson: 87).

As is standard in early Christian exegesis, Egypt here represents evil, sin and the passions, the way of life that must be abandoned. This passage refers implicitly to ascetical fasting, which is discussed explicitly elsewhere in the treatise (Jaeger 7.1:28; cf. *De orat. Dom.* 2, PG 44:1168D-75A), and also to the broader ascetical effort to purify oneself from vice. Gregory represents the soul as a bag which must be emptied of evil so that it can be filled with good. As I have shown elsewhere, the concept of the human person as a receptacle is important in his anthropology (Harrison, 1989; 1992: chaps. 3, 5). In accordance with free choice, each person receives realities from outside into the self and is then shaped by them. The human receptacle functions badly when it is filled with passions and material pleasures. In the *Life of Moses*, this is explained by analogy to the brick mold used by the Hebrew slaves in Egypt, which must be continually filled and emptied and refilled again with earth, thus requiring endless labor yet never remaining full (Jaeger 7.1:50). The Fourth Homily on the Beatitudes expresses the same idea through an image taken from Proverbs: "A cask with holes is the occupation with the pleasures of sense" (Prov 23:27, LXX). That is, the soul acts like a broken container when more and more pleasures are poured into the abyss of desire, yet it is never filled (PG 44:1244B-C). In contrast, as explained in the treatise *On the Soul and the Resurrection*, when the human receptacle is filled with virtue and divine life as intended by its Creator, it is always full and at the same time always expanding to receive more (PG 46:105A-C). This is a classic formulation of Gregory's doctrine of eternal growth in communion with God.[3]

The Cappadocian's allegorical images of food and sexuality are closely tied to the receptacle concept and thus also to each other. The next section of the manna passage in the *Life of Moses*, which explains what the food from above is, illustrates how this occurs:

> You no doubt perceive the true food in the figure of the history. The bread which came down from heaven is not some incorporeal thing. For how could something incorporeal be nourishment to a body.... Neither plowing nor sowing cultivated the body of this bread, but the earth which remained unchanged was found full of this divine food, of which the hungry partake. This miracle teaches in anticipation the mystery of the Virgin. The bread, then, which was not cultivated is the Logos (Jaeger 7.1:77–78; Malherbe and Ferguson: 88).

This passage speaks of the incarnation and perhaps also the eucharist. Christ is the true food of the soul. However, the fact that the manna is uncultivated is also interpreted as a reference to the Virgin, who conceives her Son without a man's seed. Her womb, empty of any human impregnation, is filled from above with divine life. Like the stomach receiving food, it has become an image of the human person as receptacle. By implication, the ascetic, like Mary, is called to turn away from human relationships so as to be united with God, receiving him within herself. Gregory makes this point explicitly in the treatise *On Virginity*: "What happened corporeally in the case of the immaculate Mary, when the fullness of the divinity shone forth in Christ through her virginity, takes place also in every soul through a virginal existence, although the Lord no longer effects a bodily presence" (Jaeger 8.1:254; Callahan: 11). Notice that when the human receptacle is described allegorically in terms of sexuality, it has to be represented as female (cf. *De virg.* 2 and 20, Jaeger 8.1:254–55, 328). It is no accident that in his first work, *On Virginity*, and in one of his last, the great *Commentary on the Song of Songs*, Gregory chooses feminine language to speak of the human person, especially in describing our relations with God, which for him are the definitive aspect of human identity and existence. This language refers to both men and women.

However, it is important to recognize that for Gregory gender concepts function on two different levels. In its literal sense, he regards gender as a secondary and temporary feature of the human condition, which will ultimately be transcended in the age to come (*De opif. hom.* 16–17, PG 44:177D–92A; *In Cant.* 7, Jaeger 6:212–13).[4] In the treatise *On Those Who Have Fallen Asleep*, he speculates that in the resurrection human reproductive faculties may be transformed into a capacity to become impregnated with life from God and bring forth various forms of goodness from within oneself (Jaeger 9:63).[5] This suggests that although human persons can be either male or female in this world and will be neither male nor female in the next (cf. Gal 3:28), on a different level they all relate to God in a female way, as bride to Bridegroom. Thus, gender is transcended in a literal sense but still functions in a different allegorical sense.

We will return to sexual imagery later, but first let us examine another place where Gregory speaks of food, the *Fourth Homily on the Beatitudes*, which comments on the text, "Blessed are those who hunger and thirst after justice, for they shall be filled" (Mt 5:6). The central theme of this homily is desire, which is identified with hunger. Food, the object of hunger, is therefore equated with anything that a human being desires. Gregory begins by observing that bodily loss of appetite indicates an illness caused by bad juices in the stomach, and that once these juices are purged through the appropriate medicine, health is restored together with appetite. Appetite, therefore, is good, since it is necessary to eating and food is necessary to health. However, people may choose to eat either a healthy diet or an unhealthy one (PG 44:1232C–33C). In this medical analogy, bodily functions parallel the workings of the soul. The point is that desire is essential to spiritual life, but it is important that the ascetic desire what is good and turn away from evil.

In Gregory's view, the human person is a receptacle incomplete in itself which lives, as it were, by ingesting being from outside, as the body receives food and the soul participates in divine life. It follows that desire, the drive to attract what is outside and draw it into oneself, is central to human existence. Natural hunger, which craves food the body needs, is good and also limited, whereas an extension of that hunger into an insatiable quest for luxury, wealth, ostentation and sensual pleasure, which go beyond real need, pervert it into a reprehensible passion. The homily explains this through an allegorical interpretation of the devil's words tempting Christ to turn stones into bread (Matt 4:3). Bread is intended by the Creator to feed the body, but luxuries are inedible stones since they do not meet genuine needs. Here, Gregory recommends ascetical fasting but in moderation. He is clear that both hunger and food are themselves good. After all, as he observes, Christ as human being hungered and ate in the normal human way (PG 44:1236D-40C).

After making these somewhat obvious ascetical points about fasting and turning from passions and pleasures to virtues, the homily explores some more theological and mystical dimensions of the same issues. Citing a text to which he alluded in the Prologue to the *Commentary on the Song of Songs*, he speaks of Christ's hunger:

> What is this food that Jesus is not ashamed to desire? After his conversation with the Samaritan woman he says to his disciples: My food is to do the will of my Father [cf. John 4:34]. But the will of the Father is manifest, who wills that all human persons be saved and come to a knowledge of the truth [1 Tim 2:4]. Now if such a one reaches out to save us and our life becomes his food, we have learned for what the hungry condition of soul is useful. What is it, then? Let us hunger for our salvation, let us thirst for the divine will, which is indeed that we be saved (PG 44:1240C-D).

For Gregory, God does not live by participation in other realities as his intelligible creatures do; he is good and does not receive goodness from outside through grace as is the case with human beings (Balás). Therefore, the divine nature does not have the character of a receptacle, nor is it naturally hungry. These ontological structures highlight the significance of what is said in the passage we have just quoted. They indicate that the Father desires human salvation only out of gratuitous love. And in obedience to this salvific will, the Son condescends through the incarnation to hunger for human souls; he seeks to draw them into himself as members of his Body. This constitutes a striking reversal of the ordinary ontological pattern. Given this fact, our homilist concludes that we should follow Christ's example in hungering for God's will, whatever it is, for it surely aims at our salvation (cf. *De orat. Dom.* 4, PG 44:1161D-64C).

This text has an important parallel in the *Tenth Homily on the Song of Songs*, where the bride is represented as inviting the Bridegroom to eat the fruit of her garden (cf. Cant 4:16). Gregory expresses wonder at her boldness since the One to whom she offers food from her own resources is none other than the Creator of all things who provides food to every creature and descends in the incarnation as bread from heaven to give life to the world. Her banquet table is a garden of living trees, which are understood allegorically as follows:

> We indeed are the trees, and the food offered to him is our soul's salvation. While feasting on our life, he said, "My food is that I do the will of my Father" [John 4:34]. The aim of the divine will is clear since "he wishes all human persons to be saved and come to a knowledge of the truth" [1 Tim 2:4]. This salvation then is the food prepared for him. The fruit is our free will which itself gives God our souls to pluck, as it were, on a small branch. The

bride first enjoyed the apple's sweet fruit, saying: "And his fruit was sweet to my taste" [Cant 2:3]. Then she herself becomes the lovely, sweet fruit offered to the husbandman for his enjoyment (Jaeger 6:303-304; McCambley: 190-91).

Here, the same verses from John and 1 Timothy are cited and explain more fully the ontological reversal in the *Fourth Homily on the Beatitudes*. The fruit which Christ eats is "our" life and free will, and these are identified with the person of the bride herself, who here represents the authentic Christian. Gregory refers back to an earlier point in the *Commentary* in order to make reference to her spiritual journey: The Bridegroom became her food in the form of an apple. Because she has already received him within herself in this way, she is able in return to offer herself to him as fruit. This imagery depicts the mutual indwelling of Christ and the soul in an intense and graphic way. It is this mutuality, founded upon God's descent in the incarnation, which enables him, as it were, to hunger and feed on his creatures, as well as become their true food.

The next passage in the *Fourth Homily on the Beatitudes* explains that to hunger for justice is to desire all the virtues. Gregory develops the common Cappadocian theme of the unity of virtue, inherited from the philosophical tradition (Horn). It is necessary to seek all forms of goodness, since "any one form of virtue, divorced from the others, could never by itself be a perfect virtue" (PG 44:1241C-D). He supports this assertion with a philosophical argument, but he also indicates that here, as elsewhere, Scripture is expressing the whole by the part. The example he gives is of divine names. When God is called Lord, or the One who is, or compassionate, all his other names are implied as well (PG 44:1241B-44A). This illustration has special significance since the status of divine names is a central issue in Gregory's theology.[6] For him they denote God's attributes and activities. Among the more important of these attributes are the virtues, as we have seen, which intelligible creatures come to possess through participation in God.

Gregory's philosophical argument is that the virtues occur together since virtue and vice are polar opposites: a virtue cannot genuinely be present together with the vice opposed to one of the other virtues. This line of reasoning may appear unconvincing, since in concrete human experience such conflicting combinations of one virtue and another vice often do occur. In the treatise *On Perfection*, Gregory acknowledges that this kind of combination does occur, but he describes it as a civil war between good and evil within the self. This inner conflict cannot end until the good wins a definitive victory and evil is completely eliminated (Jaeger 8.1:180-81), perhaps only in the next life. Thus, his affirmation of the unity of virtue needs to be understood as referring to his escatological vision of full human participation in the divine and as grounded in the unity of God, whose attributes the virtues are (*De opif. hom.*, PG 44:184D; *In Cant.* 15, Jaeger 6:466–69.; *De mort.*, Jaeger 9:62–66).

The homily then contrasts pleasures, which can only be enjoyed intermittently, with virtue, which can be exercised and thus enjoyed in all situations and which is always satisfying but never sating because it is infinite. "The possession of virtue," Gregory says, "once it is firmly established, is neither circumscribed by time nor limited by satiety." Therefore, those who hunger for it are always filled and at the same time always desire more (PG 44:1241B-45C; Graef: 126–28). Infinity, which characterizes God in contrast to created beings, is another major theme in Gregory's theology (Henessy; Mühlenberg; Barmann; Brightman; Harrison, 1992: chap. 1). What he says here implies that virtue is divine life. This theme is also closely linked to eternal growth, which is at issue from here to the end of the homily. Desire and fulfillment both can be unending, since what occurs is an ever-increasing participation in the infinite. In conclusion, he explicitly equates God or Christ with virtue and real food as the object of desire:

> It seems to me that through the ideas of virtue and justice the Lord proposes himself to the desire of his hearers. For he became for us wisdom from God, justification, sanctification and redemption, but also bread descending from heaven and living water. . . . For if, as the Psalmist says, one has truly tasted the Lord [cf. Ps 34:8], that is, if he has received God into himself, he is filled with him for whom he has thirsted and hungered, as he has promised who said, I and the Father will come and will make our abode with him [cf. John 14:23]. The Holy Spirit, of course, had already been indwelling there before (PG 44:1245C-48A; Graef: 128–29).

The homily ends by imagining what would happen to the body if it functioned like the soul's receptacle, ever expanding as it receives more and more divine life into itself. Through assimilating its daily food, such a body would grow to greater and greater height (PG 44:1248B). The absurdity of this illustration shows the difference between the biological world, with its built-in limitations of hunger and satiety, and the intelligible world, which enjoys eternal growth through participation in the Infinite.

Let us now turn from the allegory of food to Gregory's treatment of erotic love in the *First Homily on the Song of Songs*. He says explicitly at the outset that the book must not be understood in a literal sense and that the reader must approach it with ascetic discipline. Such a person is one who has stripped off the old man with his sinful desires and actions and is clothed instead with a pure way of life, which is equated with the radiant garments Christ bore in his transfiguration. Indeed, such a one has put on

Christ himself. These garments, with which one enters the inner chamber of the chaste Bridegroom, are also identified as pure, chaste thoughts. Passionate, fleshly thoughts and earthly, irrational passions are to be rigorously excluded (Jaeger 6:14–15). Thus, to read the Song of Songs appropriately, the exegete needs to discipline thoughts and desires as does the ascetic, and must already have had considerable practice in this in order to do it effectively. (Notice that grace is also required.) The one who encounters Christ and is united to him through the Song is already clothed in him. To acquire further knowledge and experience of union with God, one must already in some measure participate in it.

Gregory develops his point about proper exegesis of the Song later in the same homily. He repeats that no fleshly and passionate person should "drag down the significance of the divine thoughts and words to beastly, irrational thoughts." Instead, he recommends a deliberate transfer of attention from the sensible to the intelligible level: "Let each person go out of himself and out of the material world. Let him ascend into paradise through passionlessness, having become like God through purity. Then let him enter into the inner sanctuary of the mysteries revealed in this book" (Jaeger 6:25; McCambley: 48). This is explained further through an allegorical exegesis of the Israelites' encounter with God at Sinai (Exodus 19). The people had to prepare themselves by washing their garments and themselves, and this is interpreted as referring to a purification of heart and thoughts. Significantly, they also had to abstain from marriage. So the exegete is required to avoid rigorously any fleshly thoughts associated with sexuality or with material things in general. However, Gregory then admits that such inproper thoughts may still appear. If this occurs, like trespassing animals at Sinai, they should be "destroyed with firmer thoughts as by stones." In addition, he says that God burns with fire every material thing that appears on the mount of theophany (Jaeger 6:25–26; McCambley: 48). Thus, as ascetical writers often observe, it may be impossible to prevent inappropriate thoughts from entering the mind, but one can and should choose immediately to reject them, and the grace of divine fire also contributes to this task by purifying the mind. Gregory is asking the Song's interpreter to discipline his thoughts in a characteristically ascetical way as he turns away from the literal to the spiritual sense of the text.

What, then, is the spiritual sense? The description of a marriage actually speaks of the human soul's union with God in love. As in the *Fourth Homily on the Beatitudes*, desire is a major theme. The reader needs to have enough spiritual maturity to experience a passionate and ever-increasing desire for the invisible and incorporeal God, since the marriage depicted is accomplished through the desire for divine beauty (Jaeger

6:38,23). Such an understanding surpasses the human capacity and comes about through grace as well as ascetical effort:

> Indeed, human understanding left to its own resources could neither discover nor absorb the Song's mystery. The most acute physical pleasure, I mean erotic passion, is used as a symbol in the exposition of the doctrine of love. It teaches us of the need for the soul to reach out to the divine nature's invisible beauty and to love it as much as the body is inclined to love what is akin to itself. The soul must transform passion into passionlessness so that when every corporeal affection has been quenched, our mind may seethe with desire for the spirit alone and be warmed by that fire which the Lord came to cast upon the earth (Jaeger 6:27; McCambley: 49).

This passage aptly describes the essential work of the ascetic, the transformation of human impulses and the re-direction of their energy away from bodily pleasure and toward God. Though this work requires great effort, it is accomplished through the grace of divine fire, which kindles love for the invisible beauty. In effect, to grasp the true, allegorical meaning of the Song, the reader must be an ascetic. Gregory asserts that the text presupposes asceticism and actually teaches it through language that appears to speak of its opposite:

> What could be more paradoxical than to make nature purify itself of its own passions and legislate and teach passionlessness in words regarded as impassioned? Solomon does not speak of the necessity of being outside of the flesh's impulses or of mortifying our bodily limbs on earth, or of cleansing our mouths of impassioned words; rather, he disposes the soul to be attentive to purity through things which appear opposite to it, and he indicates a pure meaning through impassioned words (Jaeger 6:29; McCambley: 50).

This paradox occurs because the same human drive that impels one toward bodily love can also be directed toward God, and the same human receptacle that can be filled, though ineffectively, with sensual pleasure can also be better filled with divine life. The passages we have quoted show clearly how the conscious transition from literal to spiritual meaning through allegory mirrors, presupposes, and in turn teaches and encourages the ascetic's re-direction of desire.

Gregory explains further how this allegorical method functions by comparing the words of the Song to the colors used in a portrait of the king:

> In the art of painting different colors combine to represent the subject portrayed. However, the person looking at the image created by the skillful use of colors does not linger over the colors painted on the tablet; he beholds instead only the form which the artist has shown. Thus it is with the present scripture: we should not look at the material of the colors [i.e. the words]; rather, we should behold the image of the King expressed by them in the chaste concepts. For white, yellow, black, red, blue, or any other color, are these words in their obvious appearance—mouth, kiss, myrrh, wine, bodily

limbs, bed, maidens, and so forth. The form constituted by these terms is blessedness, passionlessness, union with God, alienation from evil, and likeness to what is truly beautiful and good (Jaeger 6:28–29; McCambley: 49).

Here, our homilist seems to be saying that when the various images of the Song are read in the context of the whole poem, the structure of the overall composition shows that they truly refer to passionlessness and union with God rather than to the more obvious human erotic love. However, the comparison to a painting suggests something more. Art historians have shown that fourth-century imperial iconography played a large role in the development of Byzantine Christian iconography, and indeed the two artistic genres exhibit marked similarities of form.[7] The emperor's portrait would show not only a physical likeness of his face but even more a sense of his royal majesty and detachment and his transcendence of ordinary human concerns and attainments. For this reason, it provided an obvious example of formal beauty. It was easy for Gregory to make the step from there to the image of Christ, the heavenly King, as Christian artists surely did in the next century if not before, and as his brother Basil did when speaking of the restored divine image in the newly baptised (Neri: 604–06).

A fourth-century person would look through the colors composing a portrait of the emperor and see not the colors themselves but something that transcended them, the imperial presence as majesty. Gregory is saying that in the same way, the exegete can see the image of Christ in and through the forms of language created by the combined sensual images of the Song of Songs. In a word, he treats the book like an icon, not like a naturalistic painting. He does not focus on the surface meaning, viz. on sensual love between man and woman, but looks through it in search of the transcendent spiritual meaning, viz. of mystical union between God and the soul. Gregory's allegorical exegesis, and probably that of many other Greek fathers, is *iconic exegesis* as well as *ascetical exegesis*. This means that in turning away from the text's literal sense toward its spiritual sense, the reader is not renouncing the material substance, as it were, of the words themselves. The immaterial truth is sought in and through them, not apart from them. The sensuous language of the Song, therefore, cannot be by-passed.

Moreover, the text's words and images are not treated as a code whose meaning is exhausted by identifying the underlying concepts it is thought to translate, as may occur in some kinds of allegory. As we have seen, Gregory's writings contain recurring themes, such as the human person as receptacle, but the diverse nuances used in describing such images and their appearance in different contexts add profound depth and breadth to their meaning. As the themes recur in various texts, these nuances allow Gregory to express different facets of his understanding and enable the careful reader to learn more and more of their significance for him.[8] Thus, the Song's wealth of poetic imagery is invaluable to the Cappadocian as he seeks to convey the subtleties and depths of spiritual experience and theological understanding.

In an icon, matter is not abolished but transformed. We have seen that in Gregory's spirituality human desire and receptivity are redirected and fulfilled, not extinguished. Significantly, despite his Platonism, for him the ascetical transfer of attention and value from body to soul does not mean that the body is devalued and ultimately left behind in a Platonic manner. He says that the way of life taught in the Song is an anticipation, to the extent possible, of the condition enjoyed by the saints after the resurrection when the body is reunited with the soul in peace and does not fight against it through the passions (Jaeger 6:30–31). As Peter Brown has observed, asceticism itself does not reject the body but uses it, through fasting and chastity among other things, transforming it into an effective locus and instrument for the soul's encounter with immaterial reality. In attempting to participate as much as he or she can in this age in the mode of life characteristic of the age to come, the ascetic struggles to discover the material world as an icon mediating the intelligible. The use of allegory has a natural place in this effort.

K. M. Tharakan has written about Gregory from an interesting third-world perspective, reflecting Indian culture. He suggests that for the Cappadocian, everything sensible images the intelligible, so the creation itself as well as art is essentially allegorical (Tharakan: 48–71). Such a perspective is probably closer to that of Gregory's contemporaries than is the materialism of many unreflective Westerners today. This may help to explain why an allegorical method that is both ascetical and iconic had so much appeal to Gregory's readers in the fourth and subsequent centuries.

NOTES

[1] On the central role of theology in early Christian understandings of Scripture, beginning with the New Testament authors and continuing in the various approaches of the fathers, see Greer. On Gregory's allegory, see also Laplace: 7–13, Musurillo, Bjerre-Aspegren, Tharakan: 48–71, Canévet, and Mosshammer.

[2] *Praktikos*, Prologue and chap. 1 (Guillaumont: 492, 498).

[3] On eternal growth, see Daniélou: 291–307; McGrath, chap. 8; Mühlenberg: 152–158; Ferguson.

[4] See discussions in Daniélou: 48–60; Leys; Ladner; Alexandre; Pisi; and Harrison:1990.

[5] Cf. *De virg.* 19, Jaeger 8.1:323–24, where the same kind of spiritual childbearing is ascribed to the ascetic.

[6] Divine names were a major area of contention in the Neo-Arian controversy, and Gregory discusses them at length in the second book of his massive *Contra Eunomium*.

[7] The classic study is by Grabar.
[8] In Harrison, 1992: chap. 3, I analyze how this occurs with Gregory's perfume, light and water imagery.

WORKS CONSULTED

Alexandre, Monique.
1981 "Protologie et eschatologie chez Grégoire de Nysse." Pp. 122–69 in *Arche e telos: l'antropologia di Origene e di Gregorio di Nissa*. Ed. Ugo Bianchi and Henri Crouzel. Studia Patristica Mediolanensia 12. Milan: Università Cattolica del Sacro Cuore.

Balás, David L.
1966 *ΜΕΤΟΥΣΙΑ ΘΕΟΥ: Man's Participation in God's Perfections according to St. Gregory of Nyssa*. Studia Anselmiana 55. Rome: Herder.

Bardolle, M. A.
1984 "La Vie de Moïse de Grégoire de Nysse ou le temps spirituel vécu à travers l'imaginaire d'un modèle historique." Pp. 255–61 in *Le temps chrétien de la fin de l'Antiquité au Moyen Age—IIIe–XIIIe siècles*. Colloques internationaux du Centre National de la Recherche Scientifique 604. Paris: Editions du CNRS.

Barmann, Bernard C.
1966 "The Cappadocian Triumph over Arianism." Ph. D. diss. Stanford University.

Bjerre-Aspegren, Kerstin
1977 *Bräutigam, Sonne und Mutter: Studien zu einigen Gottesmetaphern bei Gregor von Nyssa*. Lund: Akademisk Avhandling.

Brightman, Robert S.
1973 "Apophatic Theology and Divine Infinity in St. Gregory of Nyssa." *GOTR* 18:97–114.

Brown, Peter
1988 *The Body and Society: Men, Women and Sexual Renunciation in Early Christianity*. New York: Columbia University Press.

Callahan, Virginia Woods, trans.
1967 *Saint Gregory of Nyssa. Ascetical Works*. FC 58. Washington: Catholic University of America Press.

Canévet, Mariette
1983   *Grégoire de Nysse et l'herméneutique biblique.* Paris: Etudes augustiniennes.

Daniélou, Jean
1954   *Platonisme et théologie mystique: Essai sur la doctrine spirituelle de Saint Grégoire de Nysse.* 2d ed. Paris: Aubier.

Ferguson, Everett
1973   "God's Infinity and Man's Mutability: Perpetual Progress according to Gregory of Nyssa. *GOTR* 18:59–78.

Ford, Mary
1990   "Towards a Restoration of Allegory: Christology, Epistemology and Narrative Structure." *St. Vladimir's Theological Quarterly* 34:161–95.

Grabar, André
1936   *L'empereur dans l'art byzantin: Recherches sur l'art officiel de l'empire de l'Orient.* Publications de la Faculté des lettres de l'Université de Strasbourg 75. Paris: Belles Lettres.

Graef, Hilda C., trans.
1954   *St. Gregory of Nyssa. The Lord's Prayer. The Beatitudes.* ACW 18. Westminster, MD: Newman.

Grant, Robert M.
1957   *The Letter and the Spirit.* London: SPCK.

Greer, Rowan A.
1986   "The Christian Bible and Its Interpretation." Pp. 107–208 in *Early Biblical Interpretation.* James L. Kugel and Rowan A. Greer. Library of Early Christianity 3. Philadelphia: Westminster.

Guillaumont, Antoine, and Claire Guillaumont, ed. and trans.
1971   *Evagre le Pontique. Traité pratique, ou le moine.* SC 171. Paris: Cerf.

Harrison, Verna E. F.
1989   "Receptacle Imagery in St. Gregory of Nyssa's Anthropology." *Studia Patristica* 22:23–27.
1990   "Male and Female in Cappadocian Theology." *JTS* n.s. 41:441–71.

1992 *Grace and Human Freedom according to St. Gregory of Nyssa.* Lewiston, NY: Edwin Mellen.

Heine, Ronald E.
1984 "Gregory of Nyssa's Apology for Allegory." *VC* 38:360–70.

Henessy, James E.
1963 "The Background and Meaning of Divine Infinity in St. Gregory of Nyssa." Ph. D. diss. Fordham University.

Horn, Hans-Jürgen
1970 "Antakoluthia der Tugenden und Einheit Gottes." *JAC* 13:5–28.

Jaeger, Werner, ed.
1960– *Gregorii Nysseni Opera.* Leiden: Brill.

Ladner, Gerhart B.
1958 "The Philosophical Anthropology of Saint Gregory of Nyssa." *Dumbarton Oaks Papers* 12:58–94.

Laplace, Jean, ed.
1943 "Introduction." Pp. 5–79 in *Grégoire de Nysse. La création de l'homme.* SC 6. Paris: Cerf.

Leys, Roger
1951 *L'image de Dieu chez saint Grégoire de Nysse.* Museum Lessianum—Section théologique 44. Paris: Desclée de Brouwer.

McCambley, Casimir, trans.
1987 *Gregory of Nyssa: Commentary on the Song of Songs.* Brookline, MA: Hellenic College Press.

McGrath, Charles
1964 "Gregory of Nyssa's Doctrine on Knowledge of God." Ph. D. diss. Fordham University.

Malherbe, Abraham J., and Everett Ferguson, trans.
1978 *Gregory of Nyssa. The Life of Moses.* Classics of Western Spirituality. New York: Paulist.

Mosshammer, Alden A.
1990 "Disclosing but Not Disclosed: Gregory of Nyssa as Deconstructionist." Pp. 99–122 in *Studien zu Gregor von Nyssa und der*

christlichen Spätantike. Ed. Hubertus R. Drobner and Christoph Klock. Supplements to Vigiliae Christianae. Leiden: Brill.

Mühlenberg, Ekkehard
1966   *Die Unendlichkeit Gottes bei Gregor von Nyssa: Gregors Kritik am Gottesbegriff der klassischen Metaphysik*. Göttingen: Vandenhoeck & Ruprecht.

Musurillo, Herbert
1957   "History and Symbol: A Study of Form in Early Christian Literature." *TS* 18:357–86.

Neri, Umberto, ed.
1976   *Basilio di Cesarea. Il battesimo*. Brescia: Paideia.

Pisi, Paola
1981   *Genesis e Phthorá: La motivazioni protologiche della verginità in Gregorio di Nissa e nella tradizione dell'enkrateia*. Rome: Ateneo.

Srawley, James Herbert, ed.
1956   *The Catechetical Oration of Gregory of Nyssa*. Cambridge: Cambridge University Press.

Tharakan, Kizhakkethalakkal Mathan
1979   *The Poetic Act: An Enquiry into the Poetics of St. Basil of Caesarea and St. Gregory of Nyssa of the Universal Church*. Madras: Macmillan.

THE BODY AS DESERT IN
THE LIFE OF ST. ANTHONY

Neal Kelsey
Claremont Graduate School

ABSTRACT

The Life of St. Anthony narrates the experiences of the desert hermit Anthony as he travels in the Egyptian desert engaging in various ascetic behaviors. Of particular interest in this paper is the topographical map of the desert created by the narrative. It is proposed that this map does not correspond directly to the physical desert that Anthony inhabited. Rather, the map constructed in the narrative creates a fictive world. Three aspects of this narrative map will be investigated. First, the sequence of Anthony's movements and the topographical features of the desert described in the narrative will be summarized. Second, an analysis of Anthony's movements and the topography associated with his various dwelling places will be offered. Third, the narrative function of the spatial metaphors "inner"/"outer" ascribed to the mountain that becomes Anthony's final destination will be discussed. Finally, it will be argued that the production and ultimate signification of the spatial metaphors in the narrative are grounded in corporeality rather than rationality. That is, the spatial metaphors found in *The Life of St. Anthony* arise from basic experiences of the body in which pain, disease, and death encourage a mind-body dualism. In the latter the mind is positively signified, the body negatively signified. This sets up an image schema of a container with corresponding "inner" and "outer" qualities. This image schema becomes the basis for the signification of "inner" and "outer" in the narrative map of Anthony's desert.

1.1   *Review of the Life of Anthony.* The narrative reports that Anthony was born of well-to-do Christian parents living in Middle Egypt.[1] The narrative also reports that even as a boy growing up Anthony did not enjoy formal education, shunned the companionship of his peers, led a simple life at home, and abstained from rich foods and pleasure (1).[2] Thus, it is possible that Anthony was socialized in an environment where ascetic practices were common, though these reflections on Anthony's childhood must be read with some skepticism.[3]

The motivation for Anthony's eventual renunciation of the world is given in the opening section of the narrative. Less than six months after his parents' deaths Anthony was taking a walk and reflecting on

> how the Apostles left everything and followed the Savior; also how the people in Acts sold what they had and laid it at the feet of the Apostles for distribution among the needy; and what great hope [was] laid up in Heaven for such as these (2).

With these thoughts still circulating in his mind Anthony entered the church, and it just happened that the following passage was read from the Gospel:

> If thou wilt be perfect, go sell all that thou hast, and give it to the poor; and come, follow me and thou shalt have treasure in Heaven (2).

However, it is doubtful that this exhortation alone will provide sufficient explanation for Anthony's decision to embrace a more radical ascetic lifestyle. It is a dramatic story, but it lacks explanatory precision.

Anthony's first step, following the scriptural exhortation, was to immediately sell his property and place his sister in the care of virgins, retaining a small sum for the care of his sister. Upon hearing that he should have no concern for tomorrow, he distributed all that he had to the poor and devoted himself to the ascetic life on the outskirts of his own village (3). As he became more zealous, he eventually cut himself off from his house and relatives and devoted all his energies to the ascetic life (3). After Anthony had mastered himself, he left the outskirts of the village for the tombs, which were a considerable distance from the village (8). For about fifteen years Anthony struggled in one of the tombs with the Devil and demons. Finally, when he became annoyed by the constant crowds seeking advice and healing, he was forced to move to the Upper Thebaid (49). While he was on his way a voice insisted that if he really desired to be alone, then he should go up to the inner desert (49). It is at this juncture that Anthony finally finds himself atop the Inner Mountain (51, 91). Although the narrative is not consistent at this point, it seems that Anthony would go to the Outer Mountain, usually unwillingly, in order to engage in discussion with other people (72, 84, 89, 91).[4] Having lived a very long time, Anthony finally became sick, died, and was buried by two of his close companions (89–93).

1.2   *A Definition of Asceticism.* Before proceeding any further it is essential that a working definition of the term "asceticism" be offered. In the introduction to *Ascetic Behavior in Greco-Roman Antiquity: A Sourcebook*, Vincent L. Wimbush concluded that

> ascetic behavior represents a range of responses to social, political, and physical worlds often perceived as oppressive or unfriendly, or as stumbling blocks to the pursuit of heroic personal or communal goals, life styles, and commitments (1990b:2).

Wimbush goes on to argue that

> no one text, no one historical figure or group from antiquity, and no particular type of practice could adequately define or typify asceticism. The interplay of practice and motive and the seemingly infinite number of combinations and degrees of tension in the dynamic between practice and motive in different settings were found to be far too complex to allow any of us to be comfortable with generalizing the phenomenon from one focus or area of research (1990b:1)[5].

These arguments indicate that a shift has occurred away from understanding asceticism as a restrictive set of behaviors characteristic of particular geographical areas, periods in history, or radical and marginal elements of society. The emphasis is now on the *multiplicity* of forms, motives, and contexts in which ascetic behavior is found.

This essay likewise understands asceticism to represent a broad range of behaviors manifest in numerous combinations and arising out of complex relationships with society and self.[6] If this view is accepted, asceticism cannot be restricted to any particular geographical location, ethnic group, society, social class, religion, philosophy, or era. In other words, asceticism becomes a general phenomenon that can be found in various locations and times in both the modern and ancient worlds.

1.3   *Methodological Considerations.* The first assumption underlying this paper is that asceticism represents a complex set of behaviors occurring in various times and places in various combinations. The second assumption proceeds from the first, namely, that if we are interested in understanding asceticism, then generalizable theory is needed. In fact, it could be argued that the complexity of the present subject matter encourages the construction of generalizable theories as explanatory devices. Indeed, in most academic disciplines the complexity of the subject matter is usually one of the primary factors stimulating theoretical discourse and model building. Thus, the goal of this paper will be to present a model that offers an explanation for the motivating factors underlying the kinds of ascetic behavior seen in *The Life of St. Anthony.*

Finally, it is not suggested that the model offered in this paper will explain the motivation for all ascetic phenomena. It is unlikely that any single model can accomplish that task. However, it is felt that the model offered in this paper can explain the motivation for some types of ascetic behavior, particularly those in which the body and its functions are evaluated rather negatively.

2.0   *A Phenomenology of the Body as a Starting Point for Understanding Ascetic Behavior.* This paper will seek to demonstrate that both the ascetic behavior and certain spatial metaphors in The Life of St. Anthony arise out of basic corporeal experiences. It is assumed that corporeal experiences and expressions remain relatively constant across cultures and time. This is not to say that ascetic practices do not have cultural, geographical, sociological, political, or religious antecedents. Indeed, they do. However, ascetic practices that demonstrate a correlation with different types of environments can still be explained, at a more general level, as behaviors deriving from common corporeal themes.[7]

2.1 *Embodiment.* Human experience is embodied (Leder: 1). The perceptual organs of the body (eyes, ears, nose, mouth, and skin) shape the way in which human beings apprehend their environment. The musculoskeletal system determines how people move about in the world. The structure of the semicircular canals in the inner ear determine how people respond to acceleration and the effect of earth's gravity on the body. The speech organs (mouth, tongue, lips, nose, and larynx) determine how people communicate. From this brief summary of human physiology it becomes evident that human beings experience the world and themselves similarly because a shared embodiment cuts across their individual experiences.

However, embodied experience means more than perception, movement, and speech capabilities. The body is also the primary medium by which a rational world is produced. To put it another way, reality, as we know it, has a corporeal foundation. Our perception of and movement within the physical world generate basic meaning structures by which human experiences are understood and even abstract reasoning is organized. For example, the spatial metaphors "up/down," "in/out," "front/back," and "over/under" all have a corporeal basis. These metaphors form basic meaning structures through which other physical objects can be perceived and understood.

2.2 *How the Human Body is Experienced.* Though each human being possesses only one physical body, this body can be experienced in a number of distinct ways. The discussion to follow will organize corporeal experiences into three categories: the normal body, the abnormal body, and the alien body.[8] The following outline is offered as an organizer:

The Normal Body
    Background Disappearance
    Depth Disappearance
The Abnormal Body
    The Dys-appearing Body
    The Threatening Body
The Alien Body

2.2.1 *The Normal Body.* Upon initial reflection, one would think that the intimacy of a person's own body would make it a privileged object of perception, constantly reminding one of his or her corporeality. However, in this regard the experience of the body is quite paradoxical: Rather than being constantly in the forefront of a person's consciousness, the body is normally characterized by absence.[9] In the course of daily activities, people are simply not aware of their bodies.

2.2.1.1 *Background Disappearance.* The body normally does not appear to the consciousness of the individual, but disappears into the background. In this normal mode of experience the body is simply absent. Leder refers to this type of bodily absence as background disappearance. Specific portions of the body, or indeed the entire body, can disappear because at any given moment the entire body or parts of the body may not be the focal point of sensorimotor activities, but be relegated to the unconscious background in a person's experience (Leder: 26).

2.2.1.2 *Depth Disappearance.* Just as the external surfaces of the body are normally in a state of disappearance, so the viscera are characterized even more by lack of personal awareness and control. Leder refers to this type of bodily absence as depth disappearance. Again, this is the normal relationship of the viscera to the conscious self. Bodily functions such as breathing, heart rate, blood pressure control, liver function, and digestion occur automatically within the body apart from volitional control and awareness (Leder: 49).

This absence of the visceral organs and their functions results in some serious implications. Since the functions of the visceral body are essentially controlled through a variety of automatic, non-volitional systems, they can become perceived as having an "it can" and even an "I must" quality (Leder: 48). A person must eat, drink, excrete, breath, and sleep in order to appease the visceral signals and ensure the viability of the organism.[10] It is evident that a person can choose what to eat, how much to eat, and when to eat, but he/she *cannot* assert absolute authority by choosing not to eat without threatening the vitality of the entire organism (Leder: 48). This visceral disappearance, which is characterized by automaticity and autonomous demands, establishes a perception of the body as having a will completely separate from, and even opposed to the will of the person. These homeostatic visceral processes often find expression in psychological and ethical language as desires and lusts. Such physiological processes, and particularly their conscious signals (e.g. hunger, thirst, and sexual drive), can even become personified as alien forces that need to be combated, controlled, or suppressed.[11]

The brain and its activity also experience depth disappearance. The normally absent status of the brain provides the experiential basis for postulating an immaterial, disembodied, transcendent mind.[12]

2.2.2   *The Abnormal Body*. The phenomenological discussion of the body will now turn to the abnormal body, which includes the dys-appearing body and the threatening body.

2.2.2.1   *The Dys-appearing Body*. When the body is functioning without crisis, it is in a state of disappearance. The individual is simply not aware of the body in normal, everyday activities. As mentioned above, the depth disappearance of the viscera, combined with its automaticity and autonomous control, can produce the perception of an alien will within or associated with the body. This perception of normal visceral functions represents the first ingredient that encourages a dualistic model of the body. However, it is the dysfunctional body that captures the undivided attention of individuals and societies and results in an anxiety that produces on-going philosophical reflection. The body becomes dysfunctional when disease and pain are present; death represents bodily dysfunction *par excellence*. Leder refers to this dysfunctional state of the body as dys-appearance.[13]

2.2.2.2   *The Threatening Body*. The dys-appearing body gives rise to the threatening body. As mentioned above, the dys-appearing body arises only when disease, pain, or death are present. These phenomena reduce the body to a pitiful, disgusting, and contemptuous object that entraps the true self (soul or mind) within its fleshly prison. Death becomes the ultimate threat to the person.[14] Since knowledge of the dysfunctional and dys-appearing bodies cannot be avoided, each individual and society produces and legitimates anthropological and cosmological systems where pain, disease, and death can be meaningfully located.

2.2.3   *The Alien Body*. The normal depth disappearance of the viscera becomes the first ingredient that encourages a perception of the body as alien. Visceral functions are, for the most part, absent except for signals (e.g. hunger, thirst, and sexual drive) sent to the conscious part of the brain. However, rather than understanding these signals as normal physiological phenomena within a larger homeostatic system, they can be psychologized, and moralized. They become passions, lusts, and cravings. They are then interpreted as alien, occupying forces that disrupt the person's normal relationship with the world. They stand in opposition to the person's desires (Leder: 82). All of these experiences tend to produce a negative perception of the body as something alien. This perception of the body as alien can then be personified as Satan or demons.[15] From this analysis one can conclude that if corporeal phenomena (e.g. passions, lusts, and cravings) become personified as the Evil One, then the contempt for the motives of the Evil One, as interpreted through the body's normal functions, actually becomes a contempt for the body.

Just as the homeostatic processes and conscious signals arising from the normal functions of the visceral body produce a notion of an alien body with a will of its own, so even more the realities of the dysfunctional body. The painful, diseased, aging, and dead body becomes an alien force that stands in opposition to the desires and goals of the self, even threatening the vitality of the organism. Normal bodily absence is now replaced with abnormal bodily presence.

3.1 *Corporeal Experience as the Precursor of the Dualistic Image of the Body.* The dualistic image of the body does not simply arise out of metaphysical and epistemological concerns as a purely rational conceptualization. The line of argumentation presented in this essay has been taken in order to establish the basis for the dualistic image of the body with its negative and positive components (the body being associated with the negative and the mind with the positive).[16] Both the disappearing and dys-appearing bodies provide the ingredients for conceptualizing the body as an alien force with a contrary will. This conceptualization results in a rather negative evaluation of the body that demands further interpretation on the part of individuals and societies. At the same time, the depth disappearance (absence) of the mind promotes a conceptualization of the mind as disembodied and immaterial. These two phenomenological vectors combine to form a dualistic image of the body in which the alien body becomes devalued and condemned and the mind elevated.

The passions, lusts, and cravings of the alien body become a negative force responsible for "epistemological error, moral error, and mortality" (Leder: 127).[17] On the other hand, the mind is understood to incline toward virtue, goodness, and God.[18] However, the dualistic model of the body does not stop at simply conceptualizing negative and positive aspects. The passions of the body and the virtue of the mind are not understood as non-intersecting phenomena. On the contrary, the alien body becomes a formidable force that willfully sets out to obstruct the positive development of the mind towards virtue, goodness, and God.[19]

3.2 *The Relationship of the Dualistic Body with Image Schemata and Spatial Metaphors.* The phenomenology of the body discussed so far will now provide the foundation for moving into the second stage of this essay, namely, the thesis that spatial metaphors have a corporeal foundation. This is in contrast to other theories that view metaphors as stylistic devices or arbitrary signs.

3.2.1 *The Relationship of the Human Body to Space*. Geographical entities such as deserts, rivers, and mountains do not possess a natural organization or signification beyond the physical features available to the senses. Apart from cultural signification and mental activity, space has no intrinsic meaning. Space, as a meaningful entity, is a construction of the mind.

Different cultures have different concepts of the immediate physical world and the larger world or cosmos. However, there are certain principles of spatial construction that appear to be consistent across cultures. This consistency seems to be due to the fact that human beings are the "measure of all things." The mere presence of a human being in space automatically "imposes a schema on space" (Tuan: 36). The structure and normal upright posture[20] of the human being generate a set of spatial schemata: "up/down," "front/back," "high/low," "in/out," and "far/near."[21] Kant notes that "even our judgments about the cosmic regions are subordinated to the concept we have of regions in general, insofar as they are determined in relation to the sides of the body . . ." (Tuan: 36). As a result, many organizational schemata of the earth and cosmos are actually projections of the human body.

3.2.2 *Image Schemata*. Orientational metaphors such as "up/down," "in/out," "front/back," and "deep/shallow" are not arbitrary signs, but represent image schemata that are structured and maintained by basic corporeal experiences.[22] These image schemata provide a foundation for interpreting other experiences. Without these image schemata human experiences would appear chaotic and incomprehensible.[23] According to Johnson, image schemata are:

1. recurring patterns that arise out of bodily movement, manipulation of objects, and perceptual interactions.
2. gestalt structures consisting of parts standing in relations and organized into unified wholes, by means of which a person's experience manifests discernible order.
3. dynamic patterns that function somewhat like abstract structures of images thereby connecting up a vast range of different experiences that manifest recurring structures.
4. a part of the nervous system. They are an active array of physiological structures and processes: not a center in the brain, but an entire system that includes receptors and afferents that feed forward units and efferents (xix, 2, 20).

In addition to the above characteristics, image schemata are not fixed but continuously modified by experience (Johnson: 20). At any given moment, an image schema negotiates understanding by means of sensory information acquired from the environment and at the same time is itself modified (Johnson: 20).

From the above premises we can propose that the environment does not exist as a brute fact but is understood by means of pre-existing image schemata. There is "no 'pure' act of perception, no seeing without thinking" (Kress and Hodge: 5). The barrage of stimuli constantly bombarding the body are selectively intercepted by our senses and accorded meaning by means of image schemata.[24]

3.2.3   *Containment and Boundedness as Basic Image Schemata.* The image schema "in/out" arises out of the basic corporeal experience of boundedness. This is because the body is experienced as a three-dimensional container with the skin acting as the boundary between the outer world and the inner self. Thus, an "in/out" image schema is established by the structure and experience of the body and its relationship to the world.

Mark Johnson believes that "our encounter with containment and boundedness is one of the most pervasive features of our bodily experience" (21). The body can be perceived as both something contained (e.g. within a room, city, or clothes) and as a container within which other objects are placed (e.g. food, water, or air) or located (e.g. mind or soul). Since the mind (the real self) experiences depth disappearance, it exists as an object hidden within the body.[25] However, the dys-appearance (abnormal presence) of the body results in a negative conceptualization of the "body-as-container" so that the body becomes a prison of the mind. As a result of this corporeal foundation, an image schema evolves in which "in" becomes positively charged and "out" negatively charged.

3.2.4   *Boundedness and Metaphor Production.* The image schema "in/out" does more than simply provide a means of orienting people within their environment. As is true of all image schemata, this "in/out" schema can be projected onto other physical objects that possess boundedness (Lakoff and Johnson: 29). Indeed, even objects that do not appear to possess a notion of boundedness can be so configured. This is precisely how Anthony's Inner and Outer Mountains function. The one acts as a container for the other. From this perspective it becomes obvious that these Inner and Outer Mountains are fictive geographical features constructed by the narrative for purposes other than historical report.

4.1   *The Spatial Contours of Anthony's Journey.* The topography described in *The Life of St. Anthony* includes the Nile River, Anthony's village along the Nile, and the desert. Basically, this space is organized within the narrative in terms of horizontal and vertical distances. The initial reference point is Anthony's village on the Nile. After giving up all of his possessions, Anthony moves to the *edge* of the village. This move appears to have only a small horizontal vector since the distance is not great. Anthony's second move is into the desert a *considerable* distance from the village where he finds a tomb in which to live. Again, all of the movement is horizontal, this time further away from the village. Anthony's third move is even further into the desert but now to the *mountain* located on the *far* side of the river. There he finds an abandoned fort to inhabit. With this third move, Anthony has traveled even further into the desert. This time there are both horizontal and vertical vectors since the fort is located on a mountain. Anthony's last move is into the *inner* desert to a *very high mountain*. This move has both a horizontal vector and an accentuated vertical vector.

In summary, Anthony's movements describe a single vector that begins at the Nile River and then proceeds to move further and further away from the river while at the same time becoming more and more elevated. The movement could be summarized as a series of concentric circles each elevated above the other and forming an inverted cone.

4.2   *Spatial Metaphors in The Life of St. Anthony.* There are three variables involved in Anthony's moves—height, distance, and centeredness. The signification of height is straightforward. As mentioned above, spatial metaphors have a corporeal basis. The normal active body is *up*right whereas the inactive, sleeping body lies *down*. Serious illness also forces the body into a reclining position. The dead body is also no longer able to retain its *up*right position against the forces of gravity. Based on these corporeal experiences, "up" takes on a positive significance and "down" negative. As a result, places of higher elevation possess a positive value. Thus, Anthony regarded the Inner Mountain as his "own home," the highest elevation being associated with the premier habitation (50). The Inner Mountain is the place where Anthony finally found the solitude necessary to practice his asceticism.

The notion of horizontal distance is more complicated to analyze. In general, the value communicated seems to be negative. The primary function of distance seems to be the creation of distinct boundaries between the negative impediments of village life and the positive goals of ascetic practice. Thus, Anthony's first move (to the edge of the village) establishes an initial barrier between himself and the day-to-day activities and concerns of village life. The second and third moves (to the tomb and to the fort) create even more distance between the negative influences of society and himself, establishing an even more substantial barrier. Finally, with the fourth and final move to the Inner Mountain the distance between Anthony and his village is maximized and an ideal physical environment created for practicing his asceticism.

The increasing distance from his village also signifies an alternate social structure. Eventually the distance from the village becomes so great that an anti-world is created which stands diametrically opposed to the goals and concerns of village life. The stark contrast between the geography of the fertile Nile River Valley and the desert accentuates the notion of distance and establishes an even more severe boundary between Anthony's way of life and life in the village.

Anthony's overall movement can also be understood as a trajectory towards a positively charged center (the Inner Mountain) that is surrounded by a negatively charged outer territory. This construction of the desert corresponds with the narrator's conceptualization of the body.

4.3   *The Relationship between Physical Distance and Ascetic Practice*. The notion of physical distance in the narrative also corresponds to the thematization of the body via ascetic practices. Anthony's ascetic practices serve to create a sense of increasing distance between his outer body and inner person by making the body appear more and more alien. In this way, a stark boundary is established between his inner person and outer body.

Paradoxically, the thematization of the body via ascetic practices tends to create a positive feed-back loop in which the alien quality of the body is increased, rather than decreased. This positive feed-back loop is established mainly because the body functions as both the object of ascetic practice and the instrument through which ascetic goals are accomplished. Thus, Anthony's ascetic practices tend to aggravate and increase the presence of the disappearing body as a rebellious body that must be subdued by additional ascetic practice.

4.4   *The Relationship between the Inner and Outer Mountains and the Conceptualization of the Body*. The Inner and Outer Mountains are of particular interest because of the manner in which they parallel the narrator's conceptualization of the human body. Both the Inner Mountain and inner person (soul) are signified positively, whereas the Outer Mountain and body are negative entities. In both instances the outer entity functions as both a boundary and a container. In both instances the final destination is the most inward aspect. These parallels exist because the construction of the desert in the narrative and the conceptualization of the human body are based on the same image schema ("inner/outer") and this image schema has a corporeal basis. This means that the conceptualization of the body is actually foundational and provides the primary ingredients for the narrative map of the desert.

4.5   *The Relationship between the Social Body and the Physical Body*. Mary Douglas states that "the social body constrains the way the physical body is perceived" (1982: 65). Even though this statement expresses a truth, it is only half the truth. Indeed, Douglas' statement can be turned around by saying that in the case of Anthony, physical and social worlds are constrained by the way the body is perceived. Although there is a reciprocal relationship between the social world and the body, more stress needs to be placed on the effect that corporeal experiences have on the conceptualization of the social world. If this orientation is accepted, then we can say that the narrator's map of the desert in *The Life of St. Anthony*, with its Inner and Outer Mountains, arises from basic image schemata, of corporeal origin, that are then projected onto other objects, in this case the desert and its topography.

In the same way that the very fabric of village life appears to be possessed by an alien force that is no longer in accord with God's will, Anthony's body becomes an alien force acting contrary to his will. His anxiety concerning village life is paralleled by his anxiety about his body with all of its desires and passions. This anxiety about village life and the body also forms a positive feed-back loop, since many of the desires and passions of the body find their *telos* within the structures of village life. Anthony's renunciation of the village life removes the *telē* of many of his passions and desires but does not remove the passions and desires themselves. Thus, Anthony seeks out additional means by which the passions and desires can ultimately be subdued.

For Anthony, both village life and his body function as prisons from which he seeks escape. These social and corporeal prisons arise out of the same image schemata—boundedness and "inner/outer." Normal corporeal existence (characterized by passions, desires, suffering, and death) produces a constricting effect. In a parallel fashion, village life (characterized by birth, eating, and drinking, and eventually death) has a constricting, imprisoning effect.

Since society no longer appears to have a center (e.g. city, gods, myths, or temple) that functions to provide a structure within which Anthony's life can proceed meaningfully, all that appears now are the outward motions of village life. Anthony's response, in many ways, is similar to that of the typical Mediterranean personality. The irrelevancy of the existing social structures moved the center away from the city, temples, and their myths to the individual soul. The freedom that could not be found in society could now be found by transcending the world via a flight to the inner person.

Once the center of meaning is moved to the inner person, then the body becomes quite problematic. The body becomes not only a prison but also an impediment to the soul's progress to God. In this context ascetic practice becomes the means for disassociating the body from the inner self so that the inner self can eventually experience a pure knowledge of reality and God, unobstructed by the passions and lusts of the body. However, the more thematized the body becomes through ascetic practice the more rebellious it appears, and the more attention must be given to ascetic practice. This sequence thematizes the body even more, thus repeating the cycle (another positive feed-back loop).

5	*Conclusions and Summary.* The logical progression of this essay has moved from a phenomenology of the body, to the nature of image schemata, to metaphor production, and finally to an application of the proposed model to *The Life of St. Anthony*. This summary, however, will move in the opposite direction. It will begin with the map of the desert presented in *The Life of St. Anthony* and will end with a summary of the significance of a phenomenology of the body.

This essay has attempted to demonstrate that the map of the Egyptian desert presented in *The Life of St. Anthony* does not correspond to the actual physical topography of the desert within which Anthony traveled for two reasons: first, the author had no intention of providing the reader with a topographical map that could later be used to duplicate Anthony's actual journey through the Egyptian desert; second, the author probably did not have detailed information about Anthony's journey, nor is it likely that he had a personal and intimate knowledge of the various locations where Anthony abided. Rather, the map of the desert in *The Life of St. Anthony* is an imaginative space that was written into existence by imposing certain meaningful spatial metaphors on otherwise generic and meaningless physical entities (e.g. mountains, rivers, caves, forts).

One of the central propositions presented in this essay is the notion that the spatial metaphors used in *The Life of St. Anthony* are produced by intrinsic image schemata, namely, the schemata of "containment" (inner/outer) and "height" (up/down). It is maintained that these image schemata are structured and maintained, subjectively, by basic corporeal experiences, rather than objective intellection.

It can then be observed that the pairs of spatial metaphors ("inner/outer" and "up/down") are signified, either positively ("inner" and "up") or negatively ("outer" and "down"). A phenomenology of the body can be used at this point as a means of explaining this positive/negative signification. Like other animals, human beings have bodies. However, unlike other animals, human beings spend a great deal of time *thinking* about their bodies, mainly because both the "disappearing" and "dys-appearing" bodies create a notion of the body as an object quite distinct from the subject (self/mind). Thus, life lived in a body tends to produce a dualistic image of the person, an image comprised of two components—mind and body. Furthermore, these two components of a person are signified as positive (mind) and negative (body). This signification is not arbitrary but is based primarily on life lived in the body—a sick, painful, suffering, aging, and dying body. From these basic corporeal experiences the image schema of containment is produced and, in turn, this image schema can now produce the metaphor pair "inner/outer," where "inner" is positively signified and "outer" is negatively signified.

However, the body is more than a passive object of reflection that can be understood as a negative container. Both the "disappearing" and "dys-appearing" bodies can result in a perception of the body as both threatening and alien. Now, the body, with its passions and cravings, has become the enemy. It actively stands in opposition to the goals of the person and, for this reason, must be controlled or even combated and defeated. This orientation results in a contempt for the functions of the body, which are now either under the control of demons or personified as Satan himself. The primary weapon that is used against these personified passions and cravings of the body is extreme ascetic practice.

The basic ingredient that contributes to the signification of the body-container (outer component) as negative and the mind (inner substance) as positive is the lived experience in a body: a body that contracts diseases, feels pain, grows old, becomes decrepit, and eventually dies—a mortal body. Almost paradoxically, this exceedingly fragile, valueless body-container is visualized as containing an immortal substance (soul, spirit, inner person). This construction of the human person provides both the basic ingredients (containment) and signification of the basic pair of spatial metaphors "inner/outer."

Most religious systems, and the dualistic anthropologies inherent in them, can be explained by the existential threats of disease, aging, and death. The Apostle Paul states that death is the final enemy (1 Cor 15:26). Similarly, Heidegger points out that "dying is never simply a physical event, but of existential and ontological import" (Leder: 83). The reality of the perishable body results in the image of the body as a prison or trap within which one must struggle to gain freedom. Freedom can be gained by thematizing the body via ascetic practices in order to reinforce the barrier between the outer and inner aspects of the person. This results in a devaluation of the body and an elevation of the soul/mind.

Thus, we can conclude that the map in the narrative does not represent the actual topography of the Egyptian desert. Rather, the map of the desert plotted in the narrative is an imaginative construction that provides a map of the body and the inner person. The map of the desert in *The Life of St. Anthony* can also serve as an illustration of the various stages of ascetic life for the practicing monk, a kind of ascetic ascent. Thus, the topography described by the narrative map correlates more with the configuration of the human body and ideas about ascetic practice than with the Egyptian desert.

Objectivistic attempts to correlate the map of the desert in *The Life of St. Anthony* with the actual topography of the Egyptian desert are essentially misleading. The Inner and Outer Mountains in *The Life of St. Anthony* do not represent historical or topographical information. The mountains in the text are disconnected from the actual topography of the desert and represent, rather, fictive locations within the narrative. However, even though these narrative, fictive places exist only in the mind of the narrator and his readers, they take on the same status as actual physical entities (Merrell: 18). Thus, objects and locations within the physical and imaginary worlds begin to share in a common reality and the imaginative Inner and Outer Mountains in *The Life of St. Anthony* come to possess epistemic value for the reader. This is so because reality is not a fixed, mind-independent, historically neutral entity that is simply explicated and understood through logical manipulation of symbols to finally produce universally accepted propositions and models that correspond with "the way things really are." Reality, as it is experienced and articulated by each individual, has both objective and imaginative/subjective components that are intertwined, often blurring the distinction between the two. Analyses and descriptions that do not take this factor into consideration are limited and perhaps misleading.

Finally, an important motivating factor for the asceticism seen in *The Life of St. Anthony* is primarily derived from Anthony's corporeal experiences rather than his relationship with society. But, it does not follow that corporality will be the main motivating factor in all types of asceticism. It does seem, however, that corporality must be considered as one of the primary motivating factors in asceticism that devalues the body.

NOTES

[1] *The Life of St. Anthony* purports to be a biography of the desert hermit Anthony. Many scholars believe that it was written by Athanasius in about 357 CE, approximately one year after Anthony's death. Anthony's birth is placed by scholars in about 250 CE.

The historicity of the text is contested by scholars. That *The Life of St. Anthony* represents a reliable biography of the life of Anthony has been disputed for the following reasons. First of all, Anthony's criticism of the Arian heresy (69) seems incongruent with the lifestyle and concerns of an anchoritic desert hermit. This material seems to come from the hand of the author. In the narrative Anthony also demonstrates a rather sophisticated degree of learning regarding the theory of asceticism (16–43) and shows a familiarity with Greek philosophy and Neo-Platonism (72–80). These discourses stand in contrast with the portrayal of Anthony as one who shunned learning and books (1, 72–74). Finally, the instructions to the monks (16–43) seem to represent a monastery setting rather than Anthony's solitary desert experience.

Athanasian authorship of *The Life of St. Anthony* is also not without controversy. On the positive side, the witness of the early church Fathers supports Athanasian authorship. Jerome demonstrates acquaintance with the *Vita* in both the original and Latin versions of Evagrius. Both Gregory of Nazianzus and Palladius indicate that Athanasius was the author of *The Life of St. Anthony*. The anonymous author of *The Life of Pachomius* also reports that Athanasius was the author of the *Vita*. However, since the Reformation Athanasian authorship has been disputed. For introductory discussions of the problem of authorship see Meyer: 8–12, Gregg: 14, Chitty, 1975: vii, Brennan: 52–54, Barnard: 169–75; Bouyer: 15–27.

[2] All references to and quotations from *The Life of St. Anthony* are taken from *St. Athanasius: The Life of Saint Anthony* translated and annotated by Robert T. Meyer.

[3] Berger and Luckmann propose that people are born within pre-existing comprehensive histories and that this pre-determined social location decisively shapes a person's view of the world (130–31). They identify two stages of socialization—primary and secondary. Primary socialization corresponds with early childhood and is the means by which a child becomes a member of society. Secondary socialization is the stage in which an already socialized adult becomes inducted into new sectors of society. Primary socialization is of fundamental importance for most people and secondary socialization must conform to the patterns of primary socialization. If *The Life of St. Anthony* is reliable at this point, we see Anthony growing up in a society in which asceticism is available as a way of life.

[4] Also note that Anthony comes *down* to visit the monks in the *outer* cells (73). The structure of Anthony's Inner and Outer Mountain parallels the structure of the monastery.

[5] This conclusion becomes apparent when the content of *Ascetic Behavior in Greco-Roman Antiquity: A Sourcebook* is perused. Any narrow definition of asceticism will simply not be able to cope with the diversity of ideologies and behaviors observed in the texts found in this volume. As Wimbush points out, "the collection itself, in its diversity and organization, challenges the traditional but oft-denied assumption that asceticism is a single-issue, single-praxis phenomenon, corresponding to the traditional categories of scholarship ('Christian,' 'Jewish,' 'pagan,' and the like)" (1990b:2).

[6] I would include among ascetic behaviors dieting, vegetarianism, fasting, sexual abstinence, sexual control, sexual continence, virginity, physical retreat from society, general dissipation of the body, wearing of rough clothing, flagellation, political quietism, prayer, night vigils, martyrdom, and abstinence from bathing.

[7] In her very helpful analysis of the relationship between symbols based on the body and different social experiences, Mary Douglas states that she is "prepared to push aside from [her] analysis all the variations of political structure, industrial complexity and ecological variety." Douglas believes that her methodological approach is valid since the "range of situations which use the human body for expression are fairly limited. They derive essentially from the quality of social relations" (1982: viii). In general, I am in agreement with Douglas' methodological orientation. However, whereas her analysis begins with social structures and moves to bodily expressions, my analysis begins with corporeal experience and moves to social structures.

[8] These three categories are derived from Drew Leder's phenomenological investigation of the body in which he identifies three types of corporeal experience: the ecstatic body, the recessive body, and the dys-appearing body. The ecstatic and recessive bodies represent normal corporeal experiences whereas the dys-appearing body is associated with abnormal corporeal experiences such as disease, pain, and death. Leder discusses the alien body as a component of the dys-appearing body. I have chosen to represent the alien body as a separate category. Essentially, there are no substantive differences between Leder's organization of corporeal experiences and mine. The subsequent discussion draws on Leder's phenomenological investigations.

[9] Leder uses the term *absence* in a general sense to refer to "all the ways in which the body can *be away* from itself" (26).

[10] Even Anthony ate, but only because his body required the sustenance. As a result, it was his custom to eat by himself because of the embarrassment it caused him (45).

[11] As an example, whenever Anthony was about to eat, sleep, or provide for other basic physiological needs of the body, he would become ashamed as he thought of the spiritual nature of the soul (45).

[12] The significance of the depth disappearance of the brain and its processes will be taken up again when mind/body dualism is discussed in more detail. However, this paper is primarily interested in looking at the negative side of the dualistic model of the body.

[13] In contrast to bodily disappearance, which occurs in ordinary functioning, Leder uses the term dys-appearance to refer to the body in dysfunctional states. In the case of pain, disease, and death the body manifests itself in a *dys* state (*dys* is from the Greek prefix signifying "bad," "hard," or "ill") so that the normally *absent* body now *appears* though in a grossly abnormal presence (83–84).

[14] Berger refers to death as the "marginal situation *par excellence*" (23).

[15] Anthony states that the Enemy would suggest filthy thoughts, incite him to lust, and deceive him (5). The demons pummelled and goaded him (9). Anthony also personifies fornication as a force that is "commissioned to waylay and seduce the youth, deceive people, and trip people up" (6). Finally, Anthony states that the Evil One should be more and more despised by the monks (37).

[16] This dualistic understanding of the body has a long history in Western civilization, occurring in Plato, Augustine, medieval Christianity, and Descartes. However, this dualism is not unique to the Western world but can be found in many other cultures. In many cases the pervasiveness of this dualistic model cannot be explained by literary dependency or cultural syncretism. Rather, one must start with an anthropological model that applies a phenomenological approach.

[17] The Enemy suggests filthy thoughts to Anthony (5), masquerades as a woman (5), and causes disturbances and confusion of thought that can result in remembrance of family, fear of death, and even hatred of monks (36).

[18] Anthony works hard each day to "make himself such as one should be to appear before God—pure of heart and ready to follow" (7). Anthony encourages those who wish to follow his example to seek after things that have permanence: "prudence, justice, temperance, fortitude, understanding, charity, love of the poor, faith in Christ, meekness, hospitality" (17).

[19] The Evil One tries to incite (5), deceive (5), beguile (7), seduce (6), assail (6), and tempt the monks (6) by continually placing stumbling blocks before them (6). This barrage of attacks from the Evil One means that the body must be dealt with, sometimes harshly, if the mind is to develop properly. Thus, Anthony practices asceticism in earnest (7), girding his body with faith, prayers, and fastings (5) in order to quench the "glowing coal of temptation" (7). Anthony's body was brought under subjection (55) so that eventually he had mastered himself (8) and had become a man "guided by reason and a stable character" (14).

[20] In addition to structure and posture, human beings experience space by means of vision, touch, and bodily movement (Tuan: 12).

[21] Tuan notes that "many African and South Sea languages take their spatial prepositions directly from terms for parts of the body" (44).

[22] Lakoff and Johnson understand metaphors to arise out of an interaction of physical and cultural experiences (14). In general, I agree with their assessment. However, for the time being I would like to withhold discussion of this interaction and limit my investigation to the contribution of physical factors and how they interact with corporeal experiences.

[23] Lakoff and Johnson note that "most of our fundamental concepts are organized in terms of one or more spatialization metaphors" (17).

[24] "Psychologists of perception have shown conclusively that there is no 'pure' act of perception, no seeing without thinking. We all interpret the flux of experience through means of interpretative schemata, initial expectations about the world, and priorities of interests" (Kress and Hodge: 5). "As perceivers we select from all the stimuli falling on our senses only those which interest us, and our interests are governed by a pattern making tendency, sometimes called schema" (Douglas, 1966: 36).

[25] It should be noted here that the mind is often conceptualized as an immaterial object in dualistic models of the body.

WORKS CONSULTED

Ackermann, Robert John
    1985   *Religion as Critique*. Amherst: University of Massachusetts Press.

Athanasius
    See Gregg and Meyer.

Barnard, L. W.
    1974   "The Date of S. Athanasius' Vita Antonii." *Vigiliae Christianae* 27:169–75.

Berger, Peter L.
    1967   *The Sacred Canopy: Elements of a Sociological Theory of Religion*. Garden City, NY: Doubleday.

Berger, Peter L., and Thomas Luckmann
    1967   *The Social Construction of Reality: A Treatise in the Sociology of Knowledge*. Garden City, NY: Doubleday/Anchor.

Brennan, B. R.
    1976   "Dating Athanasius' Vita Antonii." *Vigiliae Christianae* 30:52–54.

Bouyer, P. Louis
    1978   *La Vie de S. Antoine*. Abbaye de Bellafontaine: Maine and Loire.

Brown, Peter
    1971   *The World of Late Antiquity: A.D. 150–750*. London: Thames and Hudson.
    1982   *Society and the Holy in Late Antiquity*. Berkeley: University of California Press.

1988   *The Body and Society: Men, Women and Sexual Renunciation in Early Christianity*. New York: Columbia University Press.

Brown, Richard Harvey
1987   *Society as Text: Essays on Rhetoric, Reason, and Reality*. Chicago and London: University of Chicago Press.

Chitty, Derwas J.
1966   *The Desert a City: An Introduction to the Study of Egyptian and Palestinian Monasticism Under the Christian Empire*. Crestwood, NY: St. Vladimir's Seminary Press.
1975   *The Letters of St. Anthony the Great*. Fairacres, Oxford: SLG Press.

Douglas, Mary
1966   *Purity and Danger: An Analysis of the Concepts of Pollution and Taboo*. London: Routledge and Kegan Paul.
1982   *Natural Symbols: Explorations in Cosmology*. New York: Pantheon.

Gregg, Robert C., trans.
1980   *Athanasius: The Life of Anthony and the Letter to Marcellinus*. New York: Paulist Press.

Hanna, Thomas
1970   *Bodies in Revolt: A Primer in Somatic Thinking*. New York: Holt, Rinehart and Winston.

Harpham, Geoffrey Galt
1987   *The Ascetic Imperative in Culture and Criticism*. Chicago: University of Chicago Press.

Hodge, Robert, and Gunther Kress
1988   *Social Semiotics*. Ithaca, NY: Cornell University Press.

Johnson, Mark
1987   *The Body in the Mind: The Bodily Basis of Meaning, Imagination, and Reason*. Chicago: University of Chicago Press.

Kress, Gunther, and Robert Hodge
1979   *Language as Ideology*. London: Routledge and Kegan Paul.

Lakoff, George
1988   "Cognitive Semantics." In *Meaning and Mental Representations*. Advances in Semiotics. Bloomington: Indiana University Press.

Lakoff, George, and Mark Johnson
　1980　*Metaphors We Live By*. Chicago: University of Chicago Press.

Leder, Drew
　1990　*The Absent Body*. Chicago: University of Chicago Press.

Merrell, Floyd
　1982　*Semiotic Foundations: Steps Toward an Epistemology of Written Texts*. Bloomington, IN: Indiana University Press.

Meyer, Robert T., trans.
　1950　*St. Athanasius: The Life of Saint Anthony*. Westminster, MD: Newman.

Pearson, Birger A., and James E. Goehring
　1986　*The Roots of Egyptian Christianity*. Studies in Antiquity and Christianity. Philadelphia: Fortress.

Rousseau, Philip
　1978　*Ascetics, Authority, and the Church in the Age of Jerome and Cassian*. Oxford: Oxford University Press.

Rousselle, Aline
　1988　*Porneia: On Desire and the Body in Antiquity*. Trans. Felicia Pheasant. New York: Blackwell.

Smith, Jonathan Z.
　1978　*Map is not Territory: Studies in the History of Religions*. Leiden: Brill.
　1987　*To Take Place: Toward Theory in Ritual*. Chicago: University of Chicago Press.

Tuan, Yi-Fu
　1977　*Space and Place: The Perspective of Experience*. Minneapolis: University of Minnesota Press.

Vlahos, Olivia
　1979　*Body the Ultimate Symbol*. New York: Lippincott.

Wimbush, Vincent L.
　1990a　"The Ascetic Impulse in Early Christianity: Methodological Implications of a Shift in Assumptions." Paper presented at the New Testament Seminar. Claremont, CA: The Institute for Antiquity and Christianity.

Wimbush, Vincent L., ed.
   1990b   *Ascetic Behavior in Greco-Roman Antiquity: A Sourcebook.* Studies in Antiquity and Christianity. Minneapolis: Fortress.

Glossary

Anapausis—the Greek word meaning "rest." In Manichaeism it was used to refer to the radical discipline of non-interaction, or "rest" from mental duplicity, oral defilement (both dietetic and oral), violence (broadly defined), desire, and economic and socio-political concerns demanded of the elect. Since according to many forms of ascetic piety humans become entangled in the world through their harmful action in it, the only solution is a complete stoppage of such action.

Anachōrēsis—the Greek word for "withdrawal." The monk withdraws from the normal social, religious, political and familial relationships in order to live in solitude and focus attention on contemplation and prayer as both strategy and end.

Anachōrētēs—the Greek word meaning "one who withdraws." In English the term usually used is anchorite.

Anorexia Nervosa—a Greek medical term describing a severe loss of appetite that has no apparent physical cause, but long associated with the abstinences of ascetics.

Apotaktikos—a Greek term meaning "one who renounces." It is used as a label for certain ascetic Christians in the fourth century.

Binah/Binatka—the Hebrew for "understanding"/"understanding (that comes from) you." An important theme in Qumran literature.

Boundedness—an image schema that proceeds from the basic corporeal experience of physical containment (e.g. inside/outside). On the one hand, the body can be experienced as a container within which certain things can be placed (e.g. food and water), on the other hand, out of which certain other things flow (e.g. urine, sweat, blood, saliva). At the same time, the body can be experienced as an object that can move in and out of various containers (e.g. rooms, vehicles, clothes).

Coenobitism—from the Greek terms *koinonia*, "community," *koinos*, "common," a form of ascetic practice characterized by communal lifestyle and subordination of the individual will to a shared "rule" or pattern of life. In Christian tradition the Pachomian coenobium is perhaps prototypical. (See *koinonia* below.)

Conciliar Acts—records of the proceedings of ancient Christian councils, published either as stenographic transcriptions or, more commonly, as a series of formal resolutions or "canons" whose literary form is modeled on that of the published opinions of the Roman Senate.

Deliberative Rhetoric—one of the three major types of rhetorical speech known in classical antiquity, used typically within political debates in a council or assembly. Other types of rhetorical speeches were judicial (as might be used in a court of law) and epideictic (as might be used on public commemorative occasions).

Disappearance (of the body)—the normal relationship of a healthy person's consciousness to his/her body. In the normal everyday mode of experience the body is simply absent, not perceived. This disappearance applies to the exterior body components (e.g. arms, legs, head) and interior components, or visceral organs (e.g. stomach, lungs, heart, brain). The disappearance of the exterior body is referred to as "background disappearance," while the disappearance of the visceral components of the body is referred to as "depth disappearance."

Dys–appearance (of the body)—a state in which the body is perceived as problematic because of the presence of disease, suffering, pain, old age, and death. The prefix "dys" means "bad," "hard," or "ill" in Greek. Thus, the phenomenon of *dys*appearance means that the normally *absent* body now *appears*, but in a grossly abnormal condition.

Encratite—from the Greek term *enkratēs*, "self-controlled," the term is used as a label for certain Christians of antiquity who practiced rather strict or rigorous forms of asceticism.

Enthusiasmos—Literally "having the deity within," a Greek term that describes a state of spiritual possession.

Eremetism—from the Greek term *eremia*, "solitude," a form of ascetic practice characterized by communal lifestyle and the cultivation of individual perfection. Anthony is, perhaps, the prototypical eremite in Christian tradition.

Hagneia—a Greek term referring to ritual purity, usually requiring abstinence from sexual relations for a period of time in order to approach, or to be approached by, a deity.

Halakah—in Judaism, rules of conduct based on religious law or custom, and considered to be a restatement of the Torah (the first five books of the Hebrew Bible).

Glossary

Hesychia—the Greek word meaning "quiet," or "rest." It denotes the state of ascetic stability and quiet. The quiet emerges from withdrawal from society, the stilling of the passions and focus upon ideals or goals (whether God or happiness, as among Greek philosophers and moralists).

Hodayah—a type of psalm or prayer of thanksgiving developed in the Qumram community. The term is derived from the introductory formula with which many of the compositions begin: "I thank you, O Lord," or "I thank you, my God."

Image Schemata—basic orientational metaphors that are structured and maintained by corporeal experiences. They make up that component of perception that lies within the perceiver and subsequently determines how objects and events in the physical world are perceived. They are not fixed, but are constantly modified by new information from personal experiences.

Inclusio—a literary device in which similar words or phrases appear at the beginning and end of a section of a text.

Koinōnia—from the Greek word *koinos*, "common," it is a reference to community. Often used as a technical term in the sources of Pachomian monasticism to refer to its particular system of affiliated monasteries. (See *Coenobitism* above.)

Maskil—an office in the Qumran community. It is associated primarily with the instruction of novices and members with liturgical functions.

Masochism/Masochistic Subjectivity—the term "masochism" is used here in the way Peter Berger suggests in *The Sacred Canopy*: ". . . the attitude in which the individual reduces himself to an inert and thinglike object vis-à-vis his fellowmen, singly or in collectivities or in the nomoi established by them. . . . Its key characteristic is the intoxication of surrender to another—complete, self-denying, even self-destroying" (55).

Metabolic Salvation—according to Manichaeism, a materialistic solution to the conflicts inherent in human existence, whereby a transformation and reordering of the body creates conditions for liberation from these conflicts.

Metaphoricity—the quality of a statement that has an indirect or mediated relationship to its referent. Metaphoricity is produced when the context (either immediately or culturally supplied) of a statement indicates that its significance is to be transferred from what is directly spoken of to an implied analogue.

Monachos—from the Greek word *monos*, "single," or "alone." *Monachos*, the monk, is therefore the solitary one. In the course of the fourth century in Christian tradition the term becomes a technical one in reference to many ascetic Christians who have chosen the way of withdrawal from everyday life. (See *Monastic Formation* below.)

Monastic Formation—systems employed to teach the monk the way of living in a monastery. These systems address every aspect of monastic living (daily schedule, eating habits, relationships, rules for prayer, reading, work). Special attention is given to discernment of spirits in monastic asceticism so that the nature of the demonic or angelic attack may be understood and appropriately addressed. (See *Monachos* above.)

Remnuoth—a label applied by Jerome to a third category of ascetics in Egypt he disparaged as heretical. Cassian referred to this same group as *sarabaitae*.

Social Body—the body of a person as it is understood from the perspective of the person's social attachments and relationships, as opposed to the perspective of the scientifically defined "atomic" body, separable from all social relationships. Since asceticism attempts to regulate both desire and social relationships, the social body becomes an important locus of ascetic activity.

Sōphrosynē—a Greek word most difficult to translate into English. Foucault describes this complex virtue as a "mode of relationship to self." As a male virtue, it was generally defined as moderation, self-mastery, or restraint. As a female virtue, it was generally understood as chastity.

SELECTED BIBLIOGRAPHY

The following list is designed to offer selected general and provocative guided reading for those interested in the intersection of historical, literary, rhetorical and discourse analysis, especially as applied to religious literature. It should complement the "Works Consulted" lists following each essay in this volume. For general reading suggestions on asceticism in particular, the reader is directed to W. Kaelber, "Asceticism," *Encyclopedia of Religion* (1987), ed. M. Eliade; Peter Brown's *Body and Society: Men, Women and Sexual Renunciation in Early Christianity* (1988), and to V. L. Wimbush, *Ascetic Behavior in Greco-Roman Antiquity: A Sourcebook* (1990).

Alter, R., and F. Kermode, eds.
    1987   *The Literary Guide to the Bible.* London: Collins.

Atkinson, C. W., et al., eds.
    1985   *Immaculate and Powerful: The Female in Sacred Image and Social Reality.* Boston: Beacon.

Auerbach, Erich
    1965   *Literary Language and Its Public in Late Antiquity and in the Middle Ages.* Trans. R. Mannheim. New York: Pantheon.

Bloch, M., ed.
    1975   *Political Language and Oratory in Traditional Society.* London: Academic.

Booth, W.
    1961   *The Rhetoric of Fiction.* Chicago: University of Chicago Press.

Burke, K.
    1962   *The Rhetoric of Religion.* Berkeley and Los Angeles: University of California Press.

Cameron, A.
    1991   *Christianity and the Rhetoric of Empire: The Development of Christian Discourse.* Sather Classical Lectures 55. Berkeley and Los Angeles: University of California Press.

Castelli, E.
    1991   *Imitating Paul: A Discourse of Power.* Louisville: Westminster/John Knox.

Conte, G. B.
: 1986 *The Rhetoric of Imitation*. Ithaca NY: Cornell University Press.

Eagleton, T.
: 1991 *Ideology*. London: Verso.

Foucault, M.
: 1972 *The Archaeology of Knowledge*. Trans. A. Sheridan-Smith. New York: Harper & Row.

Fowler, R., et al.
: 1979 *Language and Control*. London: Routledge & Kegan Paul.

Frye, N.
: 1982 *The Great Code: The Bible and Literature*. London: Routledge & Kegan Paul.

Gager, J.
: 1975 *The Social World of Early Christianity*. Englewood Cliffs NJ: Prentice-Hall.

Geertz, C.
: 1975 *The Interpretation of Cultures*. London: Hutchinson.

Gunn, G.
: 1979 *The Interpretation of Otherness: Literature, Religion, and the American Imagination*. New York: Oxford University Press.

Harpham, G.
: 1987 *The Ascetic Imperative in Culture and Criticism*. Chicago: University of Chicago Press.

Hobsbawn, E., and T. Ranger, eds.
: 1983 *The Invention of Tradition*. Cambridge: Cambridge University Press.

Hodge, R., and G. Kress.
: 1988 *Social Semiotics*. Cambridge: Polity.

Kennedy, G.
: 1972 *The Art of Rhetoric in the Roman World, 300 B.C.—A.D. 300*. Princeton: Princeton University Press.
: 1983 *Greek Rhetoric Under Christian Emperors*. Princeton: Princeton University Press.

Selected Bibliography

Kermode, F.
    1979   *The Genesis of Secrecy: On the Interpretation of Narrative*. Cambridge MA: Harvard University Press.

LaCapra, D.
    1985   *History and Criticism*. Ithaca NY: Cornell University Press.

Laeuchli, S.
    1965   *The Language of Faith*. London: Epworth.

McClendon, J. W., Jr.
    1974   *Biography as Theology*. Nashville: Abingdon.

Man, Paul de.
    1979   *Allegories of Reading*. New Haven: Yale University Press.

Mann, M.
    1986   *Sources of Social Power: A History of Power from the Beginning to A.D. 1760*. Vol.1. Cambridge: Cambridge University Press.

Merrill, Robert, ed.
    1988   *Ethics/Aesthetics: Post-Modern Positions*. Washington, D.C.: Maisonneuve.

Moretti, F.
    1988   *Signs Taken for Wonders: Essays in the Sociology of Literary Forms*. Trans. S. Fischer, D. Forcas and D. Miller. London: Verso.

Ong, W.
    1982   *Orality and Literacy: The Technologizing of the Word*. London: Methuen.

Ricoeur, P.
    1977   *The Rule of Metaphor*. Trans. R. Czerny et al. Toronto: University of Toronto Press.
    1981   *Hermeneutics and the Human Sciences: Essays on Language, Action and Interpretation*. Ed. and trans. J. B. Thompson. Cambridge: Cambridge University Press.

Said, E.
    1983   *The World, The Text, and the Critic*. Cambridge MA: Harvard University Press.

Ste. Croix, G. E. M. de.
    1981   *The Class Struggle in the Ancient Greek World*. London: Duckworth.

Soskice, J. M.
   1985   *Metaphor and Religious Language.* Oxford: Clarendon.

Sperber, D.
   1975   *Rethinking Symbolism.* Cambridge: Cambridge University Press.

Stock, B.
   1983   *The Implications of Literacy: Written Language and Models of Interpretation in the Eleventh and Twelfth Centuries.* Princeton: Princeton University Press.

Thompson, J. B.
   1990   *Ideology and Modern Culture.* Stanford CA: Stanford University Press.

White, H.
   1978   *Tropics of Discourse.* Baltimore: Johns Hopkins University Press.

www.ingramcontent.com/pod-product-compliance
Lightning Source LLC
Chambersburg PA
CBHW032258150426
43195CB00008BA/503